Shattered

Ralph Riegel is Southern Correspondent for Ireland's biggest newspaper group, covering the *Irish Independent*, *Sunday Independent* and *Evening Herald*. A graduate of DIT Rathmines, his work has also featured in *The (London) Independent*, *Daily Telegraph* and *Irish Examiner*. A regular contributor to RTÉ, TV3, BBC, Channel 4, Newstalk and C103FM, he already has six books to his name. Four were bestsellers and the sixth is now the focus of a Sky TV documentary. He lives in Cork with his wife and children.

Shattered

**KILLERS DO TIME,
VICTIMS' FAMILIES DO LIFE**

RALPH RIEGEL

The Collins Press

First published in 2011 by
The Collins Press
West Link Park
Doughcloyne
Wilton
Cork

© Ralph Riegel 2011

British Library Cataloguing in Publication Data

Riegel, Ralph.
Shattered : killers do time, victims' families do life.
1. Murder victims' families—Ireland—Case studies.
2. Murder victims' families—Legal status, laws, etc.
—Ireland. 3. Murder victims' families—Services
for—Ireland. 4. Violent crimes—Social aspects—
Ireland. 5. Violent crimes—Ireland—Psychological
aspects.
I. Title
362.8'8'09415-dc22

ISBN-13: 9781848891005

Typesetting by The Collins Press
Typeset in Adobe Garamond 11.5 pt
Printed in Great Britain by J F Print Ltd

Cover photographs courtesy of Shutterstock (top front) and
iStockphoto (bottom front and back)

Contents

'When all is said and done, memory is the only true companion of grief.'
Margaret Rumer Godden

This book is dedicated to all those contained within these pages, and those not mentioned here, who have tragically lost loved ones far before their time – and yet still found the courage to carry on.

Foreword

I had been working for just three years with the *Irish Independent* when I got the call to go to Wexford on a story on Friday 29 September 2000. A good friend, the *Independent*'s former South-Eastern Correspondent, Sarah Murphy, was in Kilkenny working on a suspected murder-suicide story and my then Group News Editor, Paul Dunne, decided I was needed in Wexford to follow up on several leads.

I made the journey from Cork to Duncannon and was standing on the pier, staring out at the depths of the wind-lashed waters when the full horror of what had happened began to slowly emerge. Father-of-two Stephen Byrne suspected his wife, Maeve, had been conducting an affair. The couple had been married for twelve years and Stephen Byrne was devastated by his suspicions. In a confrontation that went horribly wrong, he had stabbed her to death in the living room of their home at Cuffesgrange outside Kilkenny city. Maeve's body was later discovered lying behind a sofa in their comfortable bungalow.

Stephen – who worked as a storeman for a Kilkenny firm – had then got into his white Ford Escort car and driven south to Duncannon with his two sons, Alan (ten) and Shane (six), in the back seat of the car. We will never know if the two boys were aware of their mother's death and the impending tragedy that awaited them. Stephen was a lifelong angling fan and knew Duncannon well from his frequent fishing excursions. He had even brought his beloved boys along on some outings. His last trip here had been just two weeks earlier. Arriving at Duncannon in the early hours of the morning, Stephen drove on to the pier, paused briefly, and then accelerated into the deep water, killing both himself and his two sons.

A few hours after I arrived in Duncannon, word spread that the car had finally been located. It was lying on its roof in the mud of the seabed. Its windows had either shattered on impact or been blown out by the sheer force of the inrushing water. Divers later confirmed that there were no bodies in the car. When it was later lifted to the surface, a cuddly toy was found on the back seat. A few hours later, the first of the boys' bodies was recovered when it washed up on the strand over by the next headland.

Word of the grim discovery spread so fast that Gardaí were not able to cover the remains before a press photographer, using a long-distance telephoto lens, had taken some shots. The oft-maligned Irish media later decided that the photos were simply too distressing to be published, but the then new technology (digital SLR cameras) allowed the reporters at the scene to view the images within seconds of them having been taken.

The images are seared onto my memory as if I'd viewed them just yesterday. My abiding recollection is of the little boy's hand, partially closed into a fist, gripping grains of sand. His hand was unusually white except for red blotches on his skin that were clearly the result of exposure to salt water.

I wasn't the only person shocked that day. But I found the images – and the entire story – deeply disturbing. What was appallingly evident was that the little boy now lying on the Wexford strand had once been loved, cherished and protected. He had died at the hands of someone who had brought him into this world and who had loved him.

I didn't realise it at the time but the seeds for this book were sown that day. How, I wondered, do the families left behind cope with grief on this unimaginable scale? How do good people get on with their lives in the shadow of such terrible acts where the pain must reverberate over the years to come? Most disturbing of all, how can people who clearly once loved each other wreak such terrible pain and suffering? This book is an attempt to shed some light on those coping mechanisms.

The questions are as numerous as the grains of sand on that tragic Wexford beach. Despite all our advances in medicine, technology and civilisation, how are human beings still capable of such terrible acts? Can the pain of violent crime ever be erased? Perhaps, almost as importantly, do the families left behind believe that the Irish judicial and penal systems helped or hindered their subsequent recoveries? Are victims, as many tabloid newspapers routinely claim, still the voiceless in our society?

The gut-wrenching reality is that when the lurid media

headlines fade into history, when the court case and coroner's inquests are over, when the TV footage is filed for posterity in a video library, families still have to try somehow to pick up the pieces of shattered lives and move on. But how can they?

In the ten years since that awful day in Duncannon, I have seen at first hand the courage, dignity, compassion and Christian charity demonstrated by some families in the face of appallingly evil crimes committed against their loved ones. I have also seen the anger, frustration, loneliness and indignation provoked by families who feel badly let down by the system.

I reported on one case in the Circuit Criminal Court where a young man driving home from work was killed in a three-vehicle collision that had been caused by another young man grabbing and jerking the steering wheel of his friend's car as an alcohol-fuelled joke. The victim's mother took the stand to deliver her victim impact statement and carried a large brown paper bag with her. Everyone in the hushed courtroom wondered what on earth it contained. Her voice faltered as she tried to explain what the young man's death had done to her family. She then opened the paper bag to reveal a large framed photograph of her son and showed the silent courtroom the face of the young man whose life had been extinguished because of a moment of madness.

'This is my son. I want you to see him. This is my son,' she said in a voice shaking with emotion. The mother simply wanted everyone to know that the offence hadn't just created a new crime statistic – it had claimed a person of flesh and blood who left behind parents, siblings, friends, neighbours and workmates.

This book is an attempt to offer a voice to families deeply wounded by crimes that claimed the lives of their loved ones. It aims to explain through interviews, victim impact statements, court documents, trial reports and sworn testimony the exact depth of trauma experienced by the families of crime victims – and their experiences of the judicial, penal, Garda and government agencies that deal with such offences. It is a story of pain, anguish and loss, but illuminated by hope and the resilience of the human spirit.

The stories included have been chosen for numerous reasons – most because of the manner in which they depict the human trauma of violent crime and the depths of pain some families are forced to endure. Some families did not want to comment beyond the statements they had already made as part of the judicial process. Others stressed that they view the media and its portrayal of violent crime as part of the problem rather than as part of the solution.

Others simply want their loved ones to be remembered and lessons to be learned by society from the crimes that shattered their lives. Here are their stories.

Ralph Riegel
February 2011

1

John Butler

'You can't wash young blood off your hands'

Some crimes shatter entire families. They claim not just the life of the actual murder victim but effectively wreck the lives of those loved ones left behind. Picking up the pieces after a violent crime is difficult for all families but, in some cases, the aftermath proves as agonising as the initial loss itself. On 7 October 2002, John Butler (twenty) was shot at point-blank range as he walked to his home on Cork's northside, arm in arm with his girlfriend, Rachel. The killing was apparently sparked by a minor row just minutes earlier in a fast-food takeaway. It was as shocking as it was utterly pointless – and numbed not the Butler family but all of Cork city.

'I lost everything – I didn't just lose my son John that night. I lost my husband, Johnny, I lost my son's best friend – I lost my whole family,' said John's mother, Monica. 'And why? For what? It was totally senseless – a simple row. Some verbal abuse.' Monica does not exaggerate the impact the appalling crime had on her family. Four years after her son's killing, her husband, Johnny, found he could no longer cope with the pain and opted to take his own life. Her son's best friend, a young man who had done so much to try and help the family cope with their grief in 2002, also took his own life. Monica's health was left shattered and she ended up not being able to live in the house in which she had reared John because every nook and cranny held memories of her only child who was now lost to her.

'They took everything from me that night. The only thing I have left is my grandson, Jamie. He is eleven years old now and he will grow up without ever knowing his Daddy. He won't have John around to kick a football with him or take him for an ice cream. How can anyone ever be expected to try to cope with that?' she said.

Yet that October night initially seemed like any other night for Monica and the Butler family. There were no hints that, in one random act of senseless violence, the family would be torn apart and left, years later, still waiting for answers as to why the twenty-year-old was gunned down in such a brutal and cruel fashion.

John Butler was that night preparing to start his week's work. But first he was looking forward to a Sunday night out with his partner, Rachel. John was as shrewd in business as he was hard working. He had worked on the factory floor of a number of premises on Cork's northside including KeyTech and Apple. He was a diligent, hard-working employee and got on well with his workmates and supervisors.

But John was also ambitious to work for himself and, with the help of his father, he started a business whereby he would collect builders' waste from construction sites around Cork and bring it to the landfill dump. With the Celtic Tiger construction boom just getting into its stride, it was a business that was in great demand and John hoped to be able to focus full-time on his collection operation.

John and Rachel had a three-year-old son together, Jamie. They had met as teenagers when they were both sixteen and it had been love at first sight. They made a striking couple. Rachel was a few months older than John but, such was the maturity of the young man, it seemed to everyone that he was several years older than her. Jamie was born when John was just approaching his nineteenth birthday – but the young man displayed maturity beyond his years with the new arrival. He doted on his little boy and both friends and his family joked that he could hardly wait for the youngster to be able to walk and run so that he could play football with him. Before Jamie could even walk, John had bought his son a Manchester United strip. John was a football fanatic and had been such a good player in his own youth that he had had trials with two Premiership clubs. The Old Trafford outfit were his boyhood heroes and going to Manchester to see United was one of his greatest dreams come true. John played with Blarney United and watching football was one of his great passions. 'John was soccer mad – he was always either playing football or watching it on the telly. He adored Man United and never missed a match they played on the telly,' Monica later said. 'He was a great lad – he never gave us a moment's bother, not an ounce of trouble. He was never out of work and he always made sure he gave us a few pound for the house. That was the kind of lad he was. He was our only child and we doted on him.'

Like any teen, John also loved music but, unusually for someone of his generation, he adored Elvis Presley – one of his parents' favourite singers. That October night, John was hoping his parents, Monica and John, would oblige by babysitting the toddler. Like every young couple, the pair cherished their time alone together and going out on a Sunday evening had become their special treat. The Celtic Tiger economy had led to a boom in the construction sector and John had more work that he could handle. He would often work late between Monday and Friday and, occasionally, he would even agree to do some work on Saturdays. That made Sunday evenings with Rachel all the more special.

Their plans for the Sunday evening at hand were not extravagant – far from it. They would have a few drinks in a pub near John's home in Knocknaheeny on Cork's northside and catch up with the local news. Then maybe they would pay a visit to their favourite fast-food restaurant off Gurranabraher Road as they wandered home. John also wanted to chat with Rachel over what Christmas presents he was going to organise for Jamie – after all it was less than twelve weeks to 25 December. John's mother doted on her little grandson and, as John expected, was only too happy to babysit. But she warned her son that she wanted him home early as the following day was Monday.

'He rang me at seven p.m. to ask me would I baby-sit for him. So I took the baby off him and I told him to come home early. Myself, my husband and the baby went to bed and the phone then rang about 12.30 a.m. A nephew of mine was downstairs and he told me to get up out of bed as we were needed at the Regional [Cork University Hospital]. So my husband got up and I stayed with the baby. I just thought he would be all right in the morning. I wasn't expecting it at all – I thought it was something only minor. So, the next thing I was told it was better if I went as well. There were people waiting out in front and they brought me up to the hospital. Someone took the baby off me and I went over to see my son, John.'

John and Rachel had enjoyed a quiet, ordinary evening. They chatted about events in their lives and the prospect of Christmas on the horizon. The arrival of Jamie had made Christmas all the more special and now that he was getting older, John was determined to get the Christmas presents for his son just right. It was the type of Sunday evening routinely shared by young couples nationwide. Everything about the evening was routine until they arrived at the fast-food takeaway.

John was chatting with Rachel and apparently asked a friend to place a food order for him as he stood talking on the footpath. He waited outside for a few minutes and then walked in to collect and pay for his order.

While in the fast-food restaurant, a row broke out between several customers waiting in the queue and John. It appears that they misunderstood that an order had been placed on John's behalf earlier and that he was merely collecting his food.

The row in the fast-food restaurant apparently caused John no concerns. He left the chipper and was walking slowly home, hand in hand with Rachel, with no clue as to the horror about to engulf him. John was fit and well built – and probably would have felt confident that he could handle himself in any physical confrontation, never suspecting that he would be attacked with a weapon. It was clear he was intent on going home in peace. Had he had any inkling about being under threat, he would have accelerated his departure home with Rachel or changed his route. But John did neither and strolled on with Rachel, chatting and talking about the events of the coming week. John had barely walked 100 metres after eating his food when he was suddenly confronted by some men who appeared out of a side street, one of whom was armed with a shotgun. John heroically pushed Rachel out of the way in a bid to protect her before being blasted at point-blank range. No words were exchanged and John had no opportunity to save himself. Only a few seconds had passed between being confronted and being shot. The young man never had a chance – there was simply nowhere to run. The attackers then fled on foot, leaving horror in their wake.

Rachel, screaming for help, ran over to John who had staggered a couple of paces before collapsing from his wounds on the roadside. She cradled him in her arms as she screamed to shocked onlookers and nearby householders to call the Gardaí and get help. Witnesses at the scene were appalled to see the young woman nearly hysterical and covered in her dying partner's blood. An ambulance arrived within minutes but it was already too late. The terrible damage caused by the shotgun blast was all too apparent on the young man's prone body. The fact that John Butler had lived long enough for the paramedics to arrive was testimony to his strength, his fitness and his youth. But it simply was not enough.

In Cork University Hospital (CUH), the full nightmare of what had happened finally dawned on a dazed Monica. 'They lifted up his head and the bullet was actually popping out of his brain. I couldn't believe it. Then everything after that was a blur – just going through the rhythms, like. John was laid out – well, he was in a kind of bed. The nurses were so kind but my son was dead. We just couldn't believe he was gone.'

Even in an Ireland slowly acclimatising itself to the scourge of gun crime, this was a shocking killing. Back in 2002, Cork took great pride in its unofficial status as Ireland's safest city. The city was not immune to violence and murder, but it was mostly associated with the drugs trade and, occasionally, there was the odd murder of passion. This kind of senseless, meaningless killing was more associated with other cities – not Cork. The fact that the twenty-year-old had been gunned down apparently because of a trivial row in a fast-food restaurant was simply too hard to believe. Surely, as callers to Cork radio stations 96FM and RedFM asked, a human life was worth more than that? The truth was that the sheer pointlessness of John Butler's killing shocked everyone, including veteran Gardaí and local clerics alike. A few days later, Knocknaheeny priest, Fr Paul O'Donoghue, was asked to celebrate John's Requiem Mass as he was a long-standing friend of the family. Fr Paul had been a tower of strength for Monica and John Butler as they tried to cope with the funeral arrangements for their son in the days after the murder. But the Requiem Mass was not an easy duty for the cleric. Fr Paul struggled to cope with the tidal wave of emotions that surrounded the occasion and the appalling brutality of the crime. John was a popular and respected young man. He was a hard-working, loyal employee who was also totally dedicated to his family, which made his killing all the more sickening within the tight-knit Knocknaheeny community. Locals just could not believe what had happened on their own doorsteps.

At one point, Fr Paul broke down as the cruelty of the killing seemed to break through all protective emotional barriers. 'How can we make sense of Johnny's death? Not only have his family lost a dear loved one but they feel lost themselves,' Fr Paul said. The priest added that, judging from the spiralling number of assaults and shootings in Cork and other Irish cities, life would now seem to be worthless to some on the city streets. 'What else can you say? Johnny had his whole life in front of him and then this terrible thing happens.' Fr Paul told the congregation that Johnny had lived his short life to the full – had loved his son, Jamie, and remained close to his family. He was a keen sports fan and had adored football. 'We know now that he is safe in the cradle of God's love,' he added. In the front row of St Mary's on the Hill Church, Monica and John Butler, sitting alongside Rachel, wept uncontrollably as they said their final goodbyes to John.

The murder investigation launched by Gurranabraher Gardaí was one of the biggest ever seen in the city. Detectives under Superintendent (now retired) Mick O'Loughlin worked to try to recreate the events of the night. Gardaí conducted door-to-door inquiries, conducted almost 100 interviews and launched various appeals for information via local newspapers and radio. The Garda inquiries soon focused on several individuals. However, the tenth anniversary of John's murder is now on the horizon and no one has been convicted of the brutal killing. In an interview with Newstalk's Jonathan Healy, Monica said she felt she had to try to explain what it had been like for her and her family since 2002 as they continue their agonising wait for justice to be done.

Today, Monica Butler lives with her sister Catherine in Mahon on the opposite side of Cork city to where her son was born and raised. The memories of Knocknaheeny are simply too painful for Monica to make it her full-time home any more. She has carried her own burden since 7 October 2002 in terms of depression and heartache at the loss of her only child. Her husband, John Snr, bravely tried to carry the family through until, in June 2006, his own burden became too heavy for him. 'Myself, my husband and my son's son, who was three at the time, we didn't get no justice at all. Nothing, at all. We tried to carry on as best we could. But John [her husband] could take no more. He was fifty-nine and the nicest man you'd ever meet. John went downstairs to get a drink of water for his [prescription] tablets. He shouted upstairs to me: "Monica, I love you." It was a normal routine for us. But I knew there was something wrong. It sounded too much like a goodbye. When I got downstairs we found him out the back. I went for help. When I came back, my sister came up to me and said it was too late. She had gone out the back – he had hung himself.' For Monica, it was a devastating blow – as painful as the loss of her son four years earlier. Her family helped her through the trauma though she still struggles to cope with the emotion that comes with visiting her son and husband in their graves, side by side, at St Michael's Cemetery not far from her sister's house. 'It is not fair – it is just not fair. My grandson is left without his young father. John was taken away from him. My young son was taken away from me. My husband's son was taken away from him. My husband was then taken away from me. It wasn't just one – to me, they took my whole family. They took Jamie's family – they took his father and they took his grandfather. They have taken my family but they are walking around, getting on with their lives and building their own families. 'I have to go to St Michael's [Cemetery] if I want to see my husband and my son. They are in the graveyard. And for what? For absolutely nothing. I am a mother and I do everything in my power to get those culprits to court – because they left me with nothing. All I have is heartache and pain. The truth is that on 2 June 2006, my husband willingly gave up his battle against his grief, despair and injustice and took his own life. In his dying words, he hoped that I would be consoled with the thought that he would now be with our son. They took my whole family from me. Johnny just couldn't cope with the pain. We have got no justice.

'I have to live with what happened for every second of every minute of every hour of every day. Every step I walk I think about them. You'd be saying to yourself: "Was John calling for me as he lay dying?" The Gardaí told me it took him an hour to die. Could he be calling for me? Could he be calling for his dad? Was he calling for his baby? It is a very long time in a young life, a full hour.'

The pain is made all the greater by the fact Monica's grandson, Jamie, is now growing up without a father and grandfather who both loved him. Monica now devotes her time to trying to ensure that Jamie knows about the father who was taken away from him. It is what keeps her going – that and ensuring that the grave shared by her son and husband is immaculately maintained. 'Jamie is now eleven years old and we are still unable to explain to him about the legal issues arising from the killing of his innocent daddy. They [the killers] are not people. [They should] go up and tell the truth about the night. But it is not going to happen – people like that don't. There is no point. The way they think is he's dead, he's gone, forget about [it] – bye, bye. That's how I reckon they see it.

'But there is one thing I have to say – if they live to be one hundred, they cannot wash young blood off their hands. No matter how many times they wash their hands, they cannot wash young blood off their hands. At the end of the day, every single one of us faces being on our deathbeds – every single one of us. It may not be on their conscience now – but they are not going to be young forever. They will be on their deathbed and they will be looking at young blood on their hands – they cannot wash it off.'

Author's note: Monica Butler declined to do a specific interview for *Shattered* at the request of the Director of Public Prosecutions (DPP) in light of ongoing legal matters.

2

Celine Cawley

'Tragedy in Toytown'

It was a trial that transfixed the entire nation. For sixteen days it proved to be a Central Criminal Court drama that had virtually every single salacious ingredient possible – wealth, glamour, celebrity, betrayal, sex, lies and, ultimately, fatal violence.

Eamon Lillis' manslaughter of his wife, Celine Cawley (forty-six), provided a field day for Ireland's media who pored over every single aspect of a case, which, in its own way, seemed to reflect the malaise of the post-Celtic Tiger nation. Wealth and success, it seemed after all, wasn't such a guarantee of a happy life in modern, affluent Ireland.

For mother-of-one Celine Cawley, a former model and actress in the James Bond movie franchise who went on to launch her own hugely successful Irish TV production company, Toytown Films, her affluent middle-class dream ended in a nightmare of brutal violence. Tragically, it was at the hands of the man with whom she had chosen to build her home life.

When she first set eyes on Eamon Lillis (fifty-two), Celine immediately turned to a friend and said that he was the person she would eventually marry. That chance meeting occurred in Kinsale, County Cork, in 1990 just minutes after Celine had welcomed Ireland manager Jack Charlton to the annual Irish advertising awards that she was helping to organise. Despite the glitz and glamour of the occasion, not to mention the excitement generated by Jack Charlton's arrival fresh from his Italia '90 triumph, Celine only had eyes for Eamon Lillis.

The unlawful killing by Eamon Lillis of his wife on 15 December 2008, following an argument at their plush home at Windgate Road in Dublin's affluent Howth suburb, set in train an appalling sequence of events for three families. These events would irreparably shatter Lillis' life, that of his seventeen-year-old daughter and Celine Cawley's heartbroken family. The graphic details of the case seem to be at odds with the mundane trigger for the row, i.e. Eamon Lillis' forgetting to put out the rubbish bins for collection.

It was a case in which there was one victim but numerous casualties – especially Celine's seventeen-year-old daughter who lost both her parents, one to death and the other to a six-year-and-eleven-month prison sentence. Poignantly, the teenager – who cannot be named for legal reasons – told the Central Criminal Court in her victim impact statement that she had started the judicial process as a normal sixteen-year-old but had finished as a hardened seventeen-year-old adult. It was a case that dominated newspaper headlines for months at a time – and, when the dust finally settled, left no winners.

What was most sensational about the case was that Eamon Lillis – who appeared to have achieved a middle-class dream the envy of most Irish men – had been conducting a secret affair with a massage therapist whom he had first met through a treatment appointment made by his own wife. The 2007 Mercedes jeep, the designer clothes and the numerous foreign holidays suddenly appeared to pale in importance compared to the excitement of his unexpected affair with the pretty beauty therapist who was twenty years his junior.

The trial heard that Lillis had a passionate, sex-fuelled affair with Jean Treacy (thirty-two), a Tipperary-born beauty therapist, which began just eight weeks before his wife's death. And while Eamon Lillis and Celine Cawley outwardly had everything, their marriage was in serious trouble in the weeks before Celine's brutal death.

Celine Cawley had been attending the exclusive Howth Haven salon for treatment and was so impressed she recommended that her husband also attend for a relaxing massage. Eamon Lillis had been complaining of back problems and his wife felt a massage might help. It was a fateful recommendation. Eamon Lillis followed his wife's advice and had been attending for treatment for two years before the first sparks of a relationship developed. A native of Nenagh, Ms Treacy had been working in Dublin for some time and was already involved in a long-term relationship and had plans to marry in 2009.

She had initially worked in marketing before deciding to

study beauty therapy over a series of night courses. She began working at the Howth salon in August 2006 and, because she did facials, tans and nails, eventually met Celine Cawley. Celine had been impressed by the relief she got from light-muscle massages given by Jean Treacy and this had underpinned her recommendation to her husband to try a course of massage therapy for his own back problem. A remarkable feature of the case was that Ms Treacy bore striking physical similarities to a younger Celine Cawley.

Ms Treacy admitted to the trial that she had told other salon workers that she fancied the dapper middle-aged executive who she had eventually come to know from his visits to the treatment centre. The couple discovered they had a mutual love of dogs and their first non-salon contact came when Ms Treacy agreed to walk to Eamon Lillis' car to look at photos of his dogs (one of which was a Rhodesian Ridgeback) that he stored on his iPod. That brief meeting outside the salon seemed to change the entire dynamic between them.

'[The] rapport between us was slightly different that day,' she told the court. She also noticed that Lillis, who was slight and trim in stature, had 'really nice hands for a man's hands'. The next salon treatment session occurred the following week and, this time, Eamon Lillis asked Ms Treacy to massage the front of his shoulders. She did so but was surprised when Eamon Lillis kept his eyes wide open, most patients preferring to close their eyes during such massage treatments. Eventually, the young woman felt Eamon Lillis was staring at her so intently she almost became uncomfortable.

But then Eamon Lillis smiled and asked her what she was thinking. 'There was a certain atmosphere at that point,'

Jean Treacy explained. The young woman took his hand and placed it on her own hand where her racing pulse was easily detectable. 'Feel my pulse – this is what I am thinking,' she breathlessly told him. The following Friday, the couple's relationship became physical and Eamon Lillis bought a second phone in order to contact his young lover discreetly.

A week later, he brought her to his Rowan Hill home and they had sex. Celine was in London at the time on business for her TV production company. The couple continued a passionate affair and, in the month of December alone, Ms Treacy sent him 67 text messages and called him 66 times. Lillis rang her 19 times and sent 145 text messages. At one point, he even sent Ms Treacy a Tiffany diamond pendant with a note attached, which included the lyrics of the Beyoncé song, 'Halo'.

'At the time, I thought I was [in love] but now I realise it was more infatuation than anything else,' she said. 'We got on very well but neither of us had any idea anything would happen. I looked forward to him coming in [to the salon]. I was attracted to him, yes,' she said. The young woman described Lillis as 'refined, gentle, a bit of a dreamer – and wouldn't hurt a fly'.

Eamon Lillis had told Jean Treacy that he and Celine had already been experiencing difficulties in their marriage. The young woman said she would never have known, given that Eamon Lillis and Celine Cawley looked so good together and appeared, to most people, to be the perfect couple. At one point, Jean Treacy said that Eamon Lillis had raised the marital problems with his wife and she [Celine] had suggested that they make a list of the issues and that they would both agree to work on them. Yet, at the same time, Eamon Lillis was seeing Ms Treacy. The couple would often use his Mercedes Jeep for clandestine meetings because it had tinted glass windows. '[You weren't] looking over your shoulder – not from a seedy, sordid point of view,' the beauty therapist explained.

After Celine Cawley's death, Jean Treacy told Eamon Lillis they should not have any contact until things had calmed down – and she insisted that he should focus on his teenage daughter. At that point, she believed the story that had dominated Irish newspapers as well as the RTÉ and TV3 news bulletins that Celine had died when she and her husband had stumbled across an intruder at their luxury home and a tragic struggle erupted.

The day after Celine was found dead, Jean Treacy sent a text to him that read: 'I want you to know I still feel the exact same, OK. I'll keep those appointments for you in case you need them. I will see you at the funeral.' A later text read: 'Best of luck with everything always – you need to concentrate on (X) and what is happening to you. To do this I don't think we should have any contact till things have calmed down [for both our sakes]. I know you'll understand. Everyone is looking for a story. This is not an easy decision for me to make. Will be thinking of you every step of the way. X.'

Jean Treacy told the trial that, at that stage, she was '100 per cent sure' that Celine Cawley had died, as Eamon Lillis had claimed, during the botched burglary by a masked intruder. She had become worried about him when he did not reply to various texts she sent him on 15 December. Later, he would text her that 15 December had been: 'A horrible day, a day from hell.' He agreed with her suggestion that they not contact each other for a while – texting her on 16 December to say: 'You're probably right.' However, Eamon Lillis did ring her shortly after he was released following his arrest by Gardaí.

Some months later, in February 2009, Jean Treacy rang Eamon Lillis and they met up on three occasions. The first phone call was made by Ms Treacy when she was drunk. It was during one of these three subsequent meetings that he told her how the row with his wife had, in fact, commenced. Later, after Jean Treacy had been interviewed by the Gardaí and Eamon Lillis had been charged in connection with his wife's death, the beauty therapist was shocked to see him near both her north Dublin home and the salon where she worked. Gardaí were notified and Lillis was warned that any such movements could be interpreted as a breach of his bail terms given that Ms Treacy was now likely to be a witness in any court proceedings that would arise. He was never spotted in the locations again.

In the wake of the ending of her relationship with Lillis, Jean Treacy explained some of her final contacts with the father-of-one. 'Did I miss something, had anyone else seen it? I was trying to get a sense of him. I was just needing to get [some] closure. I wanted to get a sense but didn't want to ask him straight out what had happened,' she said.

Lillis initially denied to Gardaí that there was anything amiss in his marriage but later admitted to the affair with Jean Treacy. However, he insisted it had absolutely nothing whatsoever to do with his wife's death. Gardaí told him he had been spotted several times with Ms Treacy, including purchasing a coat at Brown Thomas and shopping at the

Pavilion Centre in Swords. He simply told Gardaí it had been 'a mid-life crisis'. He denied that he was envious of the fact Ms Treacy was due to marry another man, stressing: 'I don't do jealous.'

Jean Treacy was engaged to get married – and it was clear that this fact did matter to Eamon Lillis. Gardaí searched his Rowan Hill home and had found a handwritten note carefully stored in a bedside locker. Lillis insisted that it was simply the outline for a short-story idea – and he had a second story idea about a dog in similar such notes. But, in later questioning, he admitted that the doomed love affair note had been based in part on his own experience. The note read: 'She will get that wedding dress, she will marry Keith next June, she will send out the invites in January, you will never be with her properly, the only way you can be with her is to live here, think of the positive in the relationship, you will never take her to France, she will never share your bed, you are running out of time!!!'

Jean Treacy's evidence to the trial was sensational – and revealed the trivial nature of the dispute that had triggered the fatal row. 'He [Lillis] basically said that that morning Celine asked him take out the rubbish and that he had forgotten,' Jean told the trial. Celine – described by Lillis as 'a fighter, a tough nut' – is alleged to have verbally tackled her husband about the oversight. 'She said he was a terrible husband and useless,' Ms Treacy recalled. The verbal row escalated into a physical fight, which ended when, Lillis told his young lover, Celine had slipped and fallen on the patio, striking her head which bounced 'like a beach ball'.

Lillis told her that his wife had bitten his finger but the

couple, to protect their daughter, had agreed to say that the row was, in fact, a burglary so as to explain the cuts and bruises each bore. Lillis had insisted to Ms Treacy that he had no idea his wife was seriously injured.

Gardaí later found bloodstained clothes in a suitcase in the attic of the Rowan Hill home. These included a pair of worn blue jeans which were heavily bloodstained on the legs and crotch area, a pair of white socks, a pair of black outdoor gloves and a pair of striped boxer shorts. The clothing was all contained in a black refuse sack, which had then been placed inside a black suitcase. Gardaí also found a man's watch in the house, which had been cleaned but, on forensic examination, was discovered to have tissue and blood in its links. A search of the house also revealed a brick, carefully wrapped in a tea towel, which was in the kitchen.

The pain of these revelations was apparent from the opening day of the trial in Dublin's new criminal courts complex on Parkgate Street. Celine's elderly father, James, visibly paled in court as the details of the case slowly but sensationally emerged. When Eamon Lillis took to the stand to give evidence on Friday 22 January, it was simply too much for Mr Cawley who broke down in tears and had to be comforted by his children. Celine's brother, Chris, at one point put his face in his hands and wept as the details of how his sister died were outlined to the court. Celine's sister, Susanna, battled to hide her shock as she tried to comfort her elderly father. At times, James Cawley closed his eyes during the evidence – it was all too painful, too terrible to comprehend.

It had all seemed so different when Gardaí first responded to reports of an aggravated robbery at Windgate Road at 10.04

a.m. on 15 December 2008. Dublin fire brigade controller Kevin Moran received a 999 phone call from Eamon Lillis about an attack by a masked intruder. 'My wife has been attacked . . . a guy attacked my wife in the back of the house, Rowan Hill, on the summit of Howth.' When questioned by the controller, Lillis said he thought Celine was still alive. 'I think she is still breathing.' But, having been urged by the controller to check his wife, Lillis said he didn't think she was breathing now. He insisted that he had been attacked by the masked intruder and had suffered injuries to his head and face.

Lillis had offered investigating Gardaí a dramatic account of the home invasion. Lillis said that he had driven the couple's only child to school that morning. He had then taken their dogs for a walk and, when he returned to the house, had spotted the masked intruder. 'That was when I saw him on top of Celine,' Lillis told Gardaí. He reacted as any protective and outraged husband would – charging at the masked man. 'You f***ing b*****ks,' Lillis claimed he roared – only to be confronted by the man wielding a brick. Lillis tried to protect himself – but all the while the masked intruder remained eerily silent. The man – described by Lillis as in his twenties or thirties – was wearing a black balaclava, jeans, a dark jacket and backpack. Following the confrontation, the man ran off – and Eamon Lillis said he broke off the pursuit to return to tend his injured wife.

The trial would later hear that, in reality, it was Eamon Lillis himself who was involved in the fatal struggle with his wife. When the struggle ended with Celine falling to the ground and bleeding from head injuries, Lillis returned to the house where he changed his clothes. As his wife lay dying, he sat in the house before finally ringing 999.

Lillis later admitted that he had lied about the masked intruder. There had been no one else at the plush home that day except Eamon Lillis and Celine Cawley. The couple had had a row which sparked the physical confrontation. Eamon Lillis said that, when the verbal row moved out onto decking to the rear of their home, his wife slipped and banged her head on a brick on the ground. It was the State's case that the injuries Celine suffered were more consistent with having been struck once on the head – and then twice more on the back of the head.

In gripping evidence, Eamon Lillis said that the verbal row with Celine that morning escalated into a physical confrontation during which she had struck out at him with a brick following an accidental fall. The row erupted when Celine accused him of not doing the tasks he was supposed to around the house ranging from attending to the rubbish bins and putting out bird feed. He told her to 'feck off' at which point she got angry. Eamon Lillis said he turned away from her and then his wife appeared to trip and fall. When he looked again, she was rubbing the back of her head and had picked up a brick. He inquired whether she was OK.

'She said: "What do you care?" She was very angry. She thrust the brick at me,' he added. As the verbal row immediately re-erupted, Eamon Lillis said the dispute was now: 'vocal and nasty. I went up to her and thrust the brick at her and said: "Why don't you shove this where the sun don't shine?" I jabbed her in the shoulder with my finger.' At this point, he claimed that his wife lashed out. 'I don't think she meant to hit me but she caught me on the side of my face.' After a brief tussle in which the brick tore off Eamon Lillis' fingernail, Celine Cawley screamed. The couple fell to the ground and: 'She grabbed my hand and bit my finger.' Eamon Lillis said he only hit his wife once on the forehead to get her to stop biting into his finger. 'I didn't use that much force on her.'

When the row calmed, Eamon Lillis said he cradled his wife's head in his lap until she sat up and asked what they were going to do now? Eamon Lillis said his wife was bleeding from the head but seemed to be OK. He did not think she was seriously injured. The couple then discussed the excuse of a failed burglary in a bid to explain the cuts and scratches to their daughter who was due home from school in the afternoon. He said he then spent several minutes cleaning up, going inside the house, only to return outside and discover his wife lying motionless on the ground.

'She was lying mostly on her back, legs and arms facing sideways. I called her name. I knelt down beside her, shook her chin and she didn't wake up,' Eamon Lillis added. He then ran to dial '999' and decided to stick with the story they had agreed about an intruder at their home.

Deputy State Pathologist Dr Michael Curtis explained that it was believed Celine died from loss of blood aggravated by an inability to breathe while lying face down on the decking. The problem was further complicated by the fact Celine – a former model – had become clinically obese with her weight likely to have been a factor in her respiratory crisis.

Tragically, had Celine received prompt medical attention, she could most likely have survived. 'Such a posture, particularly in an obese woman, would have splintered her diaphragm, dangerously impairing her ability to breathe,' Dr Curtis explained. '[But] in the absence of brain injury and inter-cranial bleeding, it is probable her life may have been saved if she had received prompt medical treatment.' Dr Curtis also wondered whether the head injuries sustained by Celine Cawley could have been suffered in a fall. 'I think the one on the right frontal temporal region and the one on the left at the back are at sites not typical of injuries due to a fall.'

The trial ultimately revolved around the issue of whether there was any intent to kill – and the jury acquitted Eamon Lillis of the murder of his wife. However, they convicted him of her manslaughter. His barrister, Brendan Grehan SC, said Lillis 'is extremely sorry and regretful for what happened on that fateful day and for his subsequent behaviour'. Mr Grehan also said that Lillis was now fearful for the consequences of his actions on his daughter's future life.

When Eamon Lillis was convicted of manslaughter, there were no celebrations in court. He later received a prison sentence of six years and eleven months for his crime. Perhaps the most moving comment was from his own seventeen-year-old daughter who said that while she could forgive him for having had an affair, she could not forgive him for the lies he had told.

Celine's sister, Susanna, was equally scathing for what Lillis' lies had done to their entire family and, in particular, Celine's elderly father, James. Susanna, whose husband, Andrew Coonan, sat in the gallery to offer her support, had prepared the family's victim impact statement. Susanna had idolised Celine and the two sisters had always been close. In a trial marked by sensational developments and high emotion, the victim impact statement would prove as harrowing as any of the evidence previously offered.

'My good-humoured, roguish, fun, compassionate and caring sister is entirely deleted from my mind. In her place, a battered, head-shaven body with 18-inch injuries, slipping in blood as she fights for her life on the patio of the house of her dreams,' she wrote. What clearly stung the family most was that they had taken in Eamon Lillis during the days after his wife's death, determined to try and comfort and support him at such a terrible time. They had fully believed his story about the masked intruder. They had also believed that he had fought the mystery man to protect Celine. Yet, just five days after Celine's death, Eamon Lillis had been arrested by Gardaí. He was ultimately charged in relation to his wife's death on 22 December 2008 before Dublin District Court – a development that was absolutely shattering for Celine's entire family.

'The treacherous lies are overwhelming – but the worst lie had to be the one told by Eamon over the intruder. Whatever about the rest of us, Dad [James Cawley] deserves to know the truth,' Susanna said. 'The lack of remorse is also hard to credit – no such apology was forthcoming. For Celine and those of us who mourn her deeply, we were utterly deprived of any dignity, spirituality or peace,' she added. Insult was added to indignity for the entire family when Celine's funeral itself became what she termed 'a media circus'.

Eamon Lillis himself moved to try and dispel some of the images of Celine created during the trial. On his express instructions, his counsel Brendan Grehan SC, took issue with some of the media reports about Celine Cawley. '[Celine was] his partner in every sense of the word – he loved her very much and he will love her for the rest of his life. She was neither a bully nor a tyrant. He will regret for as long as he lives [her death]. He is extremely sorry and regretful for what happened on that fateful day and for his subsequent behaviour.'

Mr Justice Barry White – who paid tribute to the Cawley family for the dignified manner in which they faced one of the most dramatic trials of modern times – was scathing in his description of Lillis' crime. 'Your behaviour has had a devastating effect on people of all ages – from your father-in-law who is some eighty years of age down to your own daughter who is seventeen years of age,' he said.

'You concocted a story of an intruder, with whom you grappled for your life. You even went so far as to point the finger of suspicion at an innocent man. That evidence discloses that, having injured your wife, at least you had the decency to phone the emergency services and, with their assistance, attempt to revive or resuscitate her. As far as I can see that is the only decent act or acts you did that morning,' he added.

'Considering the facts of the case and considering the cover-up, the lies and the deceit that you practiced in the immediate aftermath of the death of your wife it seems to me that, taking in account the offence itself, the appropriate sentence is ten years. Your expression of remorse rings hollow to me. I consider it to be self-serving. I respect your right to plead not guilty but consider that an offer of a plea to manslaughter – which was not forthcoming – even if it were not accepted by the DPP, would have demonstrated true contrition and true remorse.

'Your own daughter sets out how she's changed from a sixteen-year-old girl into a hardened seventeen-year-old adult. I accept that you are now fifty-two and have a previously unblemished record and that this was out of character for you although I find it hard to reconcile that with your own evidence of how you told your wife to "shove it where the sun don't shine" when referring to the brick. Balancing the gravity of the offence and your own personal circumstances, I consider the appropriate sentence to be one of seven years, dating from yesterday [Thursday],' Mr Justice White declared. The sentence was later revised to six years and eleven months taking into account the time that Eamon Lillis had spent in custody on remand.

In a direct comment on the media coverage of the case, Mr Justice White said he was taken aback by some of the reports. 'It seems to me that the media have had little or no respect for the privacy or dignity of the Cawley family,' he said. The judge particularly noted the fact that Celine Cawley's teenage daughter had mentioned in her victim impact statement that the media had been hounding her. The teen – despite the fact she could not legally be identified – was still being followed by reporters and photographers. 'I can but request that ceases – I call upon the media to respect the privacy of the Cawley family,' Mr Justice White said.

On Friday 5 February 2010, minutes after Eamon Lillis was sentenced, the Cawley family emerged from the court, pale, shaken and shattered by the events of the previous four weeks. It had been the highest-profile Irish murder trial in years and the repercussions of the case would be felt for months to come. The family hugged – drawing physical support from each other – as a horde of photographers and reporters gathered for their reaction to the trial and verdict. What the family quickly highlighted as most hurtful was the manner in which Celine had been portrayed throughout the trial – and the fact that she could have been saved even after the assault if she had received prompt medical help.

'Celine was a dynamic, kind, successful, fun-loving and caring person,' her brother Chris said in an emotionally charged tribute. 'She had a beautiful energy that lit up so many lives – the lives of family, friends, neighbours and colleagues. Celine, we love you.'

Other relatives spoke of how the Celine they knew and loved was not accurately portrayed during the trial. Celine's first cousin, Juliette Hussey, told the *Sunday Independent* that the 'real Celine' was nothing at all like the image to emerge from the lengthy trial proceedings.

'Celine was incredibly hard working and very able. She was just really good at what she did. If a woman is good at something – particularly in business – there seem to be people taking swipes. I think in this idea of a ruthless businesswoman, yes [Celine was done a disservice]. The fact of the lovely person that she was, that we all knew, there was not an opportunity at the trial for that to come out. Susanna's victim impact statement very clearly described the person we knew. That is what we will always remember – the people who were close to her,' she added.

Juliette grew up with Celine and they remained lifelong friends. They even holidayed together in France, a country which Celine grew to deeply love. Her dream came true when she was able to afford to purchase a holiday home in

Hossegor in Aquitaine, north of Biarritz and west of Dax, an old Roman spa town. 'Celine kept in touch with everyone. If anyone wanted to know what anyone else was doing they called Celine. She was great – particularly for family occasions and at Christmas. She was particularly generous not just to her own daughter but to my children and her nieces and nephews. She just made life fun – when we went to France there was such excitement at spending time with her. She was incredibly good, incredibly kind and generous to all the children. She always anticipated what they wanted to do as well. She was the one who would suggest going to the waterpark, going go-karting – things she knew would give them great enjoyment.'

The trial had other casualties. Jean Treacy effectively had to live in hiding after the day she delivered her evidence such was the determination of the tabloid media to photograph her. Ms Treacy had been brought by Gardaí into court via a secure entrance to the side of the Parkgate Street complex – and had thereby avoided the waiting media. Pointedly, she was not photographed entering or exiting the building – the only image of her being from a court artist. But, as the trial and its aftermath continued to dominate the headlines, the young woman found it impossible to return to her north Dublin home.

Eventually Gardaí had to formally warn photographers to move away from the area altogether. In her native Nenagh, her family home witnessed a steady stream of reporters and photographers calling to inquire about photos and interviews. The family eventually got their solicitor to write to reporters asking them to leave the family alone and respect their privacy. Jean Treacy for a time even lived in Northern Ireland in a bid to avoid the media. The marriage that Jean Treacy and her fiancé had planned and Eamon Lillis had so clearly worried about never subsequently took place.

In the weeks after the conclusion of the trial, it emerged that Celine had left her young daughter more than €1 million in her will. An estate worth €1.059 million was inherited by the girl when she turned eighteen in 2010. The will was written by Celine in 1993 – just over two years after she had married Eamon Lillis. On 2 March – just one month after his sentencing for the manslaughter of his wife – Eamon Lillis voluntarily surrendered administration of the will to Celine's brother. Under the Succession Act (1965) he was legally prohibited from inheriting Celine's estate because he was convicted of killing her.

However, Eamon Lillis was still entitled to his share of any assets the couple jointly held and this included three properties owned by the couple – houses in Howth and Sutton in Dublin as well as the holiday villa in Hossegor in France. There was no mortgage on the couple's Howth home which is conservatively valued at €1.5 million. The Sutton house is worth an estimated €500,000 while the French holiday home is valued at more than €250,000.

The winding up of Toytown Films – the production company founded and successfully built up by Celine Cawley – is believed to have earned Eamon Lillis €300,000, all of which will be available to him on his release from prison in late 2015. One of the earliest revelations of the trial was that while Eamon Lillis earned an annual salary of €100,000 from Toytown, his wife Celine was paid €500,000.

In November 2010, it emerged that Eamon Lillis was

battling to hold on to his share in two of the homes – including the Rowan Hill house where his wife had sustained her fatal injuries. Celine's share in the home automatically reverted, via her will, to their daughter. But in a startling revelation, Mr Lillis claimed in an affidavit to the High Court that his daughter had now agreed he could return to the Howth property on his release from prison.

In the affidavit he said: 'I have discussed with my daughter what is likely to happen when I leave prison – both she and I are in agreement that I should return to the family home.' Mr Lillis was battling to keep his interest in both the Howth and Sutton properties – and the half-share he held in any assets with his late wife. The market value of both properties has since been slashed since the peak of the Celtic Tiger boom.

Mr Lillis – who is serving his sentence in Wheatfield Prison – said he is 'plagued with guilt' over his wife's death and that, having been jailed and deprived of his liberty, being stripped of his interest in the two properties would amount to a further form of punishment. 'I want to return to the family home as [my daughter's] parent, not as a sort of tenant at will or a co-owner sharing a jointly owned property with her.'

He again repeated that his wife's death was not intentional. Mr Lillis also insisted that Toytown Films was run as a joint enterprise between himself and Celine Cawley. He said that he had strong artistic skills and her forte was business operations. Mr Lillis also contended that, since the manslaughter conviction, he was 'entirely unemployable'. He insisted that his only priority now was to rebuild a relationship with his daughter.

3

Meg Walsh

'We are after living through hell'

Pretty mother-of-one Meg Walsh (thirty-five) went out socialising on 30 September 2006 with her husband, John O'Brien (forty-one). The couple followed their usual custom and went to the Woodlands Hotel near the home they shared at Ballinakill Downs in Waterford, just off the Dunmore Road. But Meg had no idea that it would prove the last night of her life.

When Meg failed to show up for work at the construction company where she worked – Meadow Court Homes – on Monday 2 October a friend was immediately concerned. When efforts to contact Meg failed, the Gardaí were notified and a huge search operation got into gear. Her car – a silver 2001 Waterford-registered Mitsubishi Carisma – was later found parked at the Uluru car park, not far from the Dunmore Road, just two miles from Waterford city centre. Calls to Meg's mobile phone went unanswered. Even more worrying, Gardaí were unable to trace a signal for Meg's mobile handset.

Within hours of the search operation being launched, Waterford Gardaí admitted they were very concerned about Meg's safety. Superintendent Dave Sheahan said the disappearance was totally out of character for Meg who was scrupulous about time-keeping and letting her friends know her movements. 'Something like this had never happened before,' he said.

Gardaí launched one of the biggest search efforts ever seen in the southeast, which ranged from 'missing' posters being put up around Waterford city and its environs to security camera footage being checked. Eventually, the search included members of the Defence Forces in Waterford, Tipperary and Kilkenny who were supported by the Irish Coastguard, Waterford Sub-Aqua Club, the Civil Defence and Waterford Coastal Rescue. Particular attention was paid to Waterford Harbour and sections of the River Suir.

After twenty-four hours, both Meg's family and senior Gardaí admitted that they now feared the worst over the woman's disappearance. By the twelfth day of the search operation, almost 500 people – mostly volunteers – were searching Waterford on a daily basis for the 35-year-old. The River Suir, Waterford Harbour, forests and beaches were all being trawled for traces of Meg. Appeals for information were published in newspapers and broadcast on radio stations.

The story of the missing woman was never off the local news bulletins or Waterford radio station, WLR FM.

On Friday 13 October, Meg's brother, James (forty), and her daughter, Sasha (seventeen), united to issue an emotional appeal for information on her whereabouts. The family had been kindly put up by the Woodlands Hotel during the search operation and the hotel hosted a special press conference which was coordinated by Superintendent Sheahan. Members of the O'Brien family were also present.

In a moving appeal, James and Sasha pleaded for any information about what had happened to Meg while admitting the previous fortnight had been 'like a horror show'. Sasha – Meg's daughter by her previous husband, Colman – said that Meg was as much her best friend as her mother.

'She was a very happy woman – she was a great mother, a great wife. She was like a sister more than a mother. We talked about absolutely everything,' Sasha said. The seventeen-year-old had been scheduled to visit with her mother in Waterford over a weekend in October – and the last time she saw Meg was on Monday 18 September when her mother seemed to be in good spirits.

'She was in great form – she was always happy and very comfortable. She was a great mother and I love her to bits and I just want her back. It was just mother/daughter talk – she was in great form. We were laughing a lot,' she added. Sasha broke down when one reporter asked her if she thought Meg was still alive. 'I hope so,' she sobbed.

Her uncle James added: 'We would dearly love to have our Mam and sister back – this situation is like a horror show. How anyone could hurt Meg in any way is beyond belief. We are desperate to find Meg – she is so important to both of us. She was our tower of strength.

'I am in bits – this is impossible. For a woman like this to disappear off the face of the earth, well, it just doesn't happen. In the absence of any contact we can only suspect that something has happened. At this stage we are appealing to any person or persons that know Meg's whereabouts to let us know where she is. We are totally in shock at Meg's disappearance and we are very concerned at this stage for her well-being. The fact that she is so reliable makes it impossible for us to imagine that she just left for somewhere without contacting one of us or her friends from work,' he added.

'[Meg] is a very thoughtful, good-natured, affectionate, outgoing bubbly girl – she loves her friends and socialising with them. She loves going out for dinner and in her leisure time likes swimming and walking.' Mr Walsh said the family was totally taken aback by the public support for the search for Meg – with busloads of volunteers travelling from north Cork each day to support the Garda search operation. 'We are shell-shocked and absolutely overwhelmed at people's generosity – we will never forget what they are doing for us and we thank them all sincerely,' he added.

John O'Brien – who did not attend the press conference – issued his own separate statement pleading for information on Meg's whereabouts. A statement made on John's behalf read: 'We would love to have Meg back with us. She is a very caring person – and has always been very good to John's parents. Please put an end to this terribly worrying time and let us know where Meg is.'

Just two days later – Sunday 15 October – the family's

worst fears were realised when a boatman spotted what he thought was a body floating in Waterford Harbour, just off Meagher Quay by the Granville Hotel. The body – which was badly decomposed – was recovered from the water and taken to Waterford morgue. A short time later it was confirmed that the remains were, in fact, those of Meg Walsh. James Walsh identified his sister's body at Waterford Regional Hospital in Ardkeen accompanied for support by Fr Paul Murphy. Mr Walsh was too devastated to speak after the grim task.

A Garda murder probe was formally launched when it emerged that Meg had died as the result of a savage assault. Detectives believe that Meg fought desperately for her life – with wounds evident to her head, face, arms, hands, neck and body. Her killer had stripped her naked before dumping her body into the River Suir wrapped in some type of material.

State Pathologist Dr Marie Cassidy performed the post mortem examination and found that Meg had died from blunt force trauma to the head. Her skull had suffered serious fractures after she was hit with a heavy, blunt object with an impact area of 5 centimetres. 'There were severe skull fractures – they were punched-out fractures of the skull,' Dr Cassidy later explained. Starkly, Dr Cassidy said that while Meg's body was in the water for some time – possibly two weeks – it is possible that she was unconscious but still alive when she was dumped into the River Suir.

Detectives suspected that Meg was killed not long after she disappeared and that her body was in the water for the best part of a fortnight. Most likely, the body broke free of its wrapping and then floated to the surface where the tide brought it close to one of Waterford's busiest quays. A

Waterford boatman, Harry Condon, spotted the body that 15 October day – and said he immediately recognised the remains as likely to be those of Meg Walsh from the colour of the hair.

In launching their murder probe, Superintendent Sheahan and Inspector Padraig Dunne admitted that they desperately needed to find key items, including the murder weapon, Meg's car keys and her mobile phone, a Motorola Razr V3 model. Gardaí were also keen to trace any movements of Meg's Mitsubishi Carisma between 7 a.m. on Sunday 1 October up until 1.03 a.m. on Wednesday 4 October.

The next week, Gardaí enlisted the services of a world-renowned dog search team from the UK. The team – which examined various sites in Waterford at the request of detectives – had been involved in some of the world's leading murder probes, including the Soham killings of Holly Wells (ten) and Jessica Chapman (ten) in August 2002 as well as a multiple murder in Nashville, Tennessee. Mark Harrison of the National Centre for Police Excellence (NCPE) admitted that one of the dogs, a spaniel named Keela, is the only animal in the world capable of detecting and following a human blood scent.

On Thursday 19 October Meg was buried, with her Requiem Mass held in the same church where she made her First Holy Communion and Confirmation almost two decades before. Meg was from Killavullen in north Cork and her brother, James, told the mourners in a packed St Nicholas' Church that such were the horrific injuries his sister sustained that her death was akin to a modern day crucifixion.

'We are after living through hell – the worst nightmare imaginable. She was taken from us in probably the most violent way imaginable. I was sitting down there looking up at that old crucifix at the back of the church and the word "crucified" actually crossed my mind. This is the gorgeous little girl that grew up with me at the foot of the Nagle Mountains. I don't know why but she idolised me – she loved me and she minded me,' he added.

'One of the rare things about her was that she had the ability to listen – Meg never talked for the sake of talking. That was her really strong point as far as I was concerned. She was my rock. It was a case of unload all your problems on me. But, sure the thing about it then, unfortunately, she felt she did not want to burden anyone with her problems. What can I say? I am just so, so proud of my sister and the way she lived her life.'

James paid a moving tribute to Meg's former husband, Colman, who had spent days helping the Garda search operation in Waterford having travelled down each day from his north Cork home. 'What can I say about Colman? I heard a Garda describing him in Waterford last week and he used the two words: "a man of integrity and substance". He spent the last fortnight in Waterford searching for our Meg.

'There isn't a whole lot more I can say about Meg – she was a gorgeous, sweet, caring woman. She was well able to speak for herself – but at this stage she cannot so I am trying to do the best I can for her. The thing about knowing Meg was that she was straight down the line – black was black, white was white, wrong was wrong, right was right. There were no half-measures.'

Meg's coffin was shouldered from the church by six specially selected people – her brother, James, relatives Robbie and Paul Walsh, her former husband Colman Keating, her friend David Maloney and her former employer, Noel Power of Meadow Court Homes.

The following day (20 October), John O'Brien was arrested by Gardaí in connection with Meg's death. He was taken to Ballybricken Garda Station in Waterford city centre and released without charge after being questioned for a period of twelve hours. Mr O'Brien – a native of Tramore, County Waterford – did not comment to a large crowd of reporters as he left the Garda Station in a car driven by a family member.

The next week, Gardaí featured Meg's disappearance and killing on RTÉ's popular *CrimeCall* programme. Detectives were determined to find Meg's keys, locate the murder weapon and identify the driver who placed Meg's Mitsubishi car in the Uluru car park. Yet, despite a massive Garda search over the following weeks and months, the murder weapon was never located.

On 21 June 2007, Gardaí arrested John O'Brien a second time and brought him to Ballybricken Garda Station. The following day (22 June) he was formally charged before Waterford District Court with his wife's murder. Mr O'Brien vehemently protested his innocence.

His trial then opened before the Central Criminal Court in Dublin in April 2008. The trial – before Mr Justice Barry White – ultimately hinged on the movements of Meg Walsh's Mitsubishi car. It was spotted on one occasion when it would have been impossible for Mr O'Brien to have driven it. The jury were also not allowed to consider a letter written by Meg Walsh in the days before her disappearance in which she wrote that she had been the victim of a serious assault. No complaint was ever made to the Gardaí about the alleged incident.

The jury acquitted Mr O'Brien by a unanimous decision on 9 May. He walked out of court an innocent man. The five-week trial had clearly been a terrible ordeal for the bus driver who appeared drawn and tired by the time it finished after nineteen days of often harrowing evidence. When the verdict was returned, Mr O'Brien sighed, closed his eyes and then shook hands with his legal team. Seconds later, he embraced his family as several of his relatives dissolved into tears in the emotion of the occasion. Mr O'Brien's mother, Sheila, wept as she hugged her son. But the family were extremely careful not to make any triumphal gestures inside the court.

Across the courtroom, Meg Walsh's daughter, Sasha, broke down in tears. Her father, Colman Keating, simply put his arm around the teen in a vain bid to comfort her. He struggled to keep his face emotionless. Meg's brother, James, fought back the tears and simply bowed his head as the verdict was returned and, after a few concluding remarks, the judge thanked the jury and sent them home.

In a brief statement afterwards, Mr O'Brien thanked the jury and all those who had supported him throughout his protestations of innocence. In a statement read out by his solicitor, Finola Cronin, on his behalf, he said he was deeply grateful to his legal team, his family and his many friends for their support which was greatly appreciated.

'John and his family would like to thank the jury for looking at the facts and reaching their decision. Thanks also to John's defence team, Mr Paddy McCarthy, Ms Iseult O'Malley and Ms Finola Cronin. Thanks to the family, friends and neighbours who supported them during the last eighteen months, especially the last four weeks. [Also] to the family who travelled from Tramore, Waterford, Wexford, Limerick and Birmingham and to their friends in Cork for all their prayers.' Mr O'Brien's statement concluded with a plea for privacy from the media to allow him to mourn for Meg and his father, who had died shortly after his wife's death.

Just minutes later, Meg's brother, James, said their entire family, including Meg's daughter, Sasha, had been absolutely traumatised by the terrible events of the past eighteen months. 'It has been very, very difficult – but we have been overwhelmed by the kindness of people,' he said. 'The whole thing is just beyond words – how could anyone do that to a kind, generous human being?'

'It has been terrible – very, very difficult. I don't think any of us thought that the whole thing would go on so long. It has been very tough. [Meg is] the last thing we think about at night and the first thing in the morning. All we can do is to depend on the memories we have of Meg – a great mother and terrific woman – to keep us going. Meg was a lovely woman, a bubbly, happy, caring woman and a great mother. We miss her terribly. As you are aware, this is an extremely difficult time and we would ask you to respect our privacy.'

In late May, John O'Brien returned to his work as a bus driver in Waterford, having taken two weeks off to recover from the undoubted ordeal of his trial. The following October, he initiated legal action to recover personal items seized from him by the Gardaí as part of the investigative process. Waterford District Court was told that while Gardaí had, following the Central Criminal Court jury verdict, returned a number of items to Mr O'Brien, they still wanted to retain a number of items. These included a bank card, a leather wallet and black purse, a Mitsubishi Carisma car registered in the name of Ms Walsh, as well as a gold necklace found on her body and a bloodstained ring. Ms Walsh had died intestate and the division of her possessions and assets was now a matter for legal decision.

The final, poignant development came the following November with the staging of an inquest by the Waterford Coroner into Meg's death. The inquest had been delayed because of the ongoing criminal matters but, with these now resolved, the inquest could be held. Waterford coroner, Dr John Goff, set the date for the inquest as 18 November 2008 with the venue being the main Waterford courthouse.

The first witness called was John O'Brien and his sworn statement, made to Gardaí, was read out to him. After the statement, no questions were put to him by legal counsel for the Walsh family.

In his statement, Mr O'Brien said that he had gone out with his wife to the Woodlands Hotel on the evening of 30 September 2006. They decided to return to their home at Ballinakill Downs at 3.30 a.m. and were accompanied by a friend, Owen Walsh, whom they had invited back to have a few more drinks.

At 5 a.m., Mr Walsh was asked if he wanted to stay over at their house given the lateness of the hour. John O'Brien told Gardaí that, as he walked past the spare room, he spotted his wife kissing Mr Walsh. At this point, Mr Walsh left and Mr O'Brien said he inquired from his wife what was going on. He informed Gardaí that Meg told him the incident would not have happened if he paid her more attention.

Mr O'Brien said he later heard his wife leaving the house – and never saw or heard from her again. Mr O'Brien said when there was no sign of his wife returning to their home that day (1 October) he rang Mr Walsh and asked did he know where she was. He also sent a text message to Meg in which he said: 'I will put it [the spare-room incident] down to a drunken kiss. Will you please call me?'

After the inquest concluded, Mr O'Brien walked, accompanied by a friend, to a waiting BMW car in the Waterford courthouse car park. He declined to comment to the assembled media beyond confirming that the past few months had been 'very tough'.

Meg's brother, James, and daughter, Sasha, had both also attended the inquest and briefly said that they hoped the killer – whoever they might be – would some day be brought to justice. James explained that the family – despite the terrible ordeal endured since 2006 – still held out hope that justice would eventually be served.

'I would like to think that whoever is responsible – at some stage – their conscience might just get at them. Maybe we can appeal to their better nature and say, look, maybe it is never too late. It is a long road without a turn – who knows? Maybe some day there will be justice done to some degree at some stage. That is all we can hope for. I think the Gardaí are still working away in the background. That is the information I have. I have every confidence in them. They are after doing an awful lot for us,' he explained.

James acknowledged that his entire family had been on edge over the impending inquest into Meg's death. 'We were dreading today, to be honest. At this stage now, it is just trying to get on with it and get it over with. All we want out of this is the truth – we want to call a spade a spade. We want the truth to be told and call it what it is.'

The judicial process had left Meg's family emotionally devastated and distraught. In an interview several weeks after the trial, Sasha Keating described the entire event as a nightmare from which the whole family simply cannot escape. 'You think when you get the date for the trial that there is finally an end in sight. But it was just the worst day of my life.'

If there was anything positive for the family, it was the support and kindness shown to them throughout by the Gardaí. 'What can you say? They were absolutely fantastic – they just couldn't do enough for us from when the search for Meg began right up to today,' James said.

The Garda file into the killing of Meg Walsh remains officially open and active. However, no one has been arrested since the Central Criminal Court trial concluded – and Gardaí are not currently following any new lines of inquiry. Garda sources admit that, without new evidence or new witnesses, that position is not likely to change.

On 8 January 2011, James Walsh and Sasha Keating held a special candlelit ceremony in Waterford to mark what would have been Meg's fortieth birthday. Both urged the killer to come forward. 'It is a crying shame that we are not celebrating instead of commemorating here today, but that's the way it is,' James said. Sasha – now a college student – said she cannot accept the fact that the person who killed her mother is still free.

4

Ann Corcoran

'A closed coffin is no way to say goodbye'

The extended family of Ann Corcoran (sixty) stood hesitantly on the steps of Cork Courthouse on Washington Street. They were clearly unfamiliar with the media throng that now accompanies most major murder cases and the post-trial reaction to sentencing. Along Washington Street that lunchtime on Wednesday 10 March 2010, shoppers and pedestrians alike paused to see what the commotion was all about.

The RTÉ and TV3 crews jostled for position, reporters hovered anxiously waiting for quotes and photographers took shots of everyone leaving the courthouse just in case it was someone of note. It was obvious to everyone that the family was clearly not happy in the limelight and wanted the media process to be over as soon as was physically possible. The trial – which had been conducted in Dublin – had been brought back to Cork for sentencing and it had been an emotionally exhausting period for Ann's extended family. That Wednesday was a cold, blustery day and people hurried about their business given the heavy showers that threatened.

First out of the confines of the early-nineteenth-century building was Ann's brother, sister-in-law and brother-in-law. Quiet, country people, they were still visibly appalled by the nature of the killing and the fact that it had been a local man who had brutally murdered their relative. They were startled by the media attention on the trial but quietly agreed to say a few words to the waiting reporters.

Ann's brother, Timothy O'Mahony, said the pain of his sister's killing still haunts the family. 'She was a very gentle person – she loved going out. She loved her dogs and her music. She liked to enjoy herself and she loved her social life. She was well liked by her neighbours,' he said. When asked about the family's opinion of Oliver Hayes, the man just convicted and sentenced for Ann's murder, he refused to be drawn. 'Not good – I knew him as a very small boy. I thought he was a nice young lad but he wasn't. It turned out so different. This pain is on us for now, on us for another while – maybe for the rest of our lives.'

Anne's brother-in-law and sister-in-law, Denis and Theresa Corcoran, said her death was still mourned by the family every single day. 'We won't get over it – not me anyway. We had a harsh situation to put up with. I am glad it is over and we will try to get back to our own lives but we won't forget it. Ann was a nice person – she had her own life. She was a very quiet person – a lovely person. She got an awful death but I hope to God, wherever she is, that she is happy. That is all I can say,' Theresa declared. Denis said the family desperately wanted to try and get on with their lives. 'We just have to put up with it now – the harm is done. He [Oliver Hayes] did the harm and he was a neighbour and all.'

Moments later, a second family group emerged from the courthouse onto the limestone steps. Several were noticeably upset by the proceedings earlier and signalled they did not want to say anything further to the media. They shook their heads when asked to comment – one politely explained they did not want to add anything to the victim impact statement read out in court just minutes earlier. But one relative, Ann's niece, Maureen O'Leary, took the opportunity to publicly welcome the life sentence handed to Oliver Hayes, which she described as justice for Ann. She also thanked the Gardaí for the professionalism of their investigation and their kindness to the family. 'We have got justice for Anne – and we want to thank the vast amount of people who came out and helped search for Anne in horrific conditions, both weather and terrain. May she rest in peace,' she said.

It had been a harrowing day for the entire family. In fact, it had been a harrowing month following a high-profile Central Criminal Court trial in which Oliver Hayes had denied the murder of Ann Corcoran but had admitted false imprisonment, five charges of theft and one charge of attempting to steal. On a 10–2 jury verdict, he was convicted of murder and received a mandatory life sentence. What had shocked people most of all was that Ann had died a violent, lonely and excruciating death for the pathetic sum of just €3,000 – €50 for each year of her life.

Her nephew, Kevin Kelly, said the violence of her death had left no member of the family untouched. His victim impact statement was one of the most touching – and yet stark – ever delivered at a murder trial outside Dublin. He captured how such a violent act impacts on a family long after the judicial proceedings are closed – and how Ann Corcoran, a quiet, kind, reserved widow, deserved far better than she received at the hands of Oliver Hayes.

'The impact of this terrible crime has changed all of our lives. Our only remaining sister and our aunt had been taken from us, forever. The beautiful memories that she shared with us about past times with our mother are no longer. The courts have heard Ann Corcoran described as a sixty-year-old woman over and over again. A stereotypical image of an ageing woman springs to mind when we hear these words but that was not true of Ann. Ann had the most wrinkle-free, smooth, porcelain skin one has ever seen. She wore little or no makeup because she did not need to – she was very beautiful.'

Kevin explained that she was more like a fifty-year-old than a sixty-year-old in her outlook. 'She walked briskly and with purpose, she always dressed so immaculately and she had a great dress sense. Ann was a devoted daughter and wife – she married Jerry when she was aged thirty-eight and shortly after, she brought her mother to live in her new home at Maulnaskimlehane [a rural area outside Bandon in west Cork]. Ann always made sure her mother was included in all social outings with herself and her new husband. She adored her mother and was her sole carer right up until her death in 2000 and likewise did the same for her husband, Jerry, up until his death in 2008. Sadly, Ann and Jerry never had any children of their own and both of them would have loved to have had them.

'Ann's passion in life were her dogs and her music. She liked nothing better than to listen to her Johnny Cash, Big Tom and Joe Dolan albums. She loved a social scene with music – she also had a great sense of humour. Her dogs were adored and better cared for than any we have ever seen. She only fed them with the best dog food type available and strictly adhered to their special dietary needs. She named her dogs with proper names like "Roy", "Trudy" and "Clive". They were more than just pets – they were like her replacement children. Ann was robbed of that chance to live out her remaining years in the comfort of her friends and family. She had a beautiful home, which was always kept in pristine condition.'

Kevin said that the family was still struggling to cope with the terrible aftermath of Ann's death and the brutal nature of how she died. 'Having to explain the word "murder" to our children was a terrible task. Trying to protect them from this was next to impossible as it was the topic of conversation from the schoolyard to the media. Ourselves and our children have, and are still, experiencing nightmares – there are times when the children don't want to sleep on their own. We also feel we were deprived of the opportunity to say a face-to-face goodbye to Ann due to the manner of her murder and subsequent disposal of her body.

'Over the past year, from the massive search for our Aunt Ann, to the funeral, right up to the trial, our family lives have been very difficult – our lives felt like they were on hold. It saddens us all very deeply to know we will never get the opportunity to carry out any plans that we made with her,' he said.

Inside the courtroom, Oliver Hayes was being prepared for a journey to prison that would see him commence a life sentence. Dressed in a sombre dark suit, white shirt and pastel tie, Hayes certainly did not look the part of a murderer. To many, he could have been an accountant or a librarian, such were his 'bookish' looks. It was hard to credit that this inoffensive-looking man had deliberately targeted the widow because he knew she lived alone and was vulnerable, attacked and abducted her simply to terrify her into giving him money. Incredibly, days after burying the widow's body in a shallow grave in an isolated forest, he had the coolness to go on a skiing holiday with his long-term girlfriend.

Hayes' final gesture to the court, before he was led away to begin his life sentence, was in keeping with the strange contradictions that surrounded the case. He offered a polite half-bow to the trial judge, Mr Justice Paul Carney, as the Prison Service officers gently led him by the arm to the holding cell for transfer back to prison. Hayes appeared in court as a shy, quiet, almost studious sort of character. In fact, the image he portrayed was the polar opposite of the type of individual normally associated with such a brutal, cruel and callous crime.

The facts of the case left the judge far from impressed, as he noted in his sentencing summation. Mr Justice Carney said the case was 'chilling' – and the death of Ann Corcoran was marked by gratuitous violence and a total lack of remorse by Hayes for the appalling act he had committed against the frail widow. He said that, in fact, Hayes had shown more concern for Ann Corcoran's dogs than he did for the woman he had battered to death, burned and then buried in a shallow grave in an isolated west Cork forest.

Hayes had decided to rob the sixty-year-old widow because he was heavily in debt and wanted cash to go on a skiing holiday in Austria with his long-time girlfriend. He knew Ann Corcoran lived alone and decided she would be a suitable target. It did not seem to matter that Ann's late husband, Jerry, had shown him great kindness over the years.

'Apart from the gratuitous violence involved, one of the chilling features of this case was the almost total lack of genuine remorse other than for the suffering [caused] to Ann Corcoran's dogs,' Mr Justice Carney said. 'As recently as last week, during the cross-examination, he [Hayes] said he was as much a victim as the unfortunate Mrs Corcoran who he had bludgeoned to death.'

The judge said that in the 'distant future', the decision over whether Hayes should be released from prison would be taken by the Parole Board and would be based on an 'intensive investigation and study' of the trial transcript, and the victim impact statement.

What had shocked everyone was the brutal death inflicted on the slightly built widow by Hayes – and the fact that the entire crime had been committed for the net gain of a pathetic €3,000. Hayes – who had been adopted at nine months of age – grew up near Mrs Corcoran's Bandon home and was known to members of her wider family. Mrs Corcoran's late husband, Jerry, had known Hayes and had worked in the same vicinity as the painter and odd-job man. Kindly, Jerry Corcoran had once given Hayes a lift for several weeks while Hayes' own car was being repaired. It was a gesture typical of Jerry Corcoran who, friends explained, didn't have a selfish bone in his body. But Jerry Corcoran – like many others in west Cork – did not know the full details of Oliver Hayes' past.

Hayes is not thought to have personally known Ann Corcoran before he attacked, abducted and killed her. He did know where she lived – possibly as a consequence of having accepted the lifts from her late husband, Jerry, many years before. He also knew she lived alone at the isolated Maulnaskimlehane farmhouse following Jerry's death in 2008 after a short illness. Hayes also knew that, in January 2009, she would be the perfect target for his scheme to address his cash crisis.

Hayes ambushed the widow when she returned to her home on the evening of 19 January. He had gone to Maulnaskimlehane just as dusk was falling. Hayes was careful to ensure he was not seen and had even walked all the way to the farmhouse to avoid having to park his vehicle anywhere nearby. As he approached the farmhouse, which is set back from the road on a short laneway, he used a ditch for cover. Hayes watched as the widow went out for a drive in her car and he made his plans for her return. He did not have to wait long as Ann had only gone on a short errand.

Hayes was waiting in the darkness when Ann returned, parked her car and then walked over to unlock her front door. Hayes sprang out of the darkness and grabbed the unsuspecting widow from behind. He bundled her into the house and immediately demanded her ATM cards and any cash she might have in the house. But if Ann Corcoran was terrified by her sudden attack, she recovered quickly and tried to fight off her assailant. Bravely, she fought back and tried to throw a vase at Hayes to frighten him away. Tragically, her efforts were in vain as Hayes overpowered her and used one of her own dog leads to tie her up and put her into the boot of her own car.

Hayes' plan was simple: he needed to scare Ann Corcoran sufficiently to cooperate fully with his plan and give him the money he wanted. He guessed that the widow would have a quantity of cash stored in her home. Hayes went on a long, meandering drive around the back roads of west Cork in the darkness in an effort to frighten Ann Corcoran. His immediate objective was to terrify her into giving him her ATM cards and her PIN numbers. When Hayes eventually stopped and opened the boot, he discovered that the plucky widow had been desperately trying to free herself from her bonds and had loosened some of her restraints. He now decided on more drastic action. He brought her back to his house at Clancool Terrace in a Bandon estate and tied her to a chair in an upstairs room, the better to force her to hand over her financial details.

Hayes' initial plan had gone awry and he decided he had no choice but to go further. Exhausted, tired, lonely and terrified, Ann Corcoran finally decided that her best option was to give Hayes what he wanted. Perhaps if he got the money he would abide by his promise and let her go. But that solution posed one major problem for Oliver Hayes: what to do next with Ann Corcoran. Ann gave Hayes the PIN numbers to her bank cards. Only then did it emerge that her bank cards were back in her home.

Hayes now faced a dilemma – he had to return to Maul-naskimlehane to get the bank cards but he could not risk moving the widow again. The trial heard that the widow was struck repeatedly with a stick by Hayes in an attempt to knock her unconscious while he got her bank ATM card and withdrew money from her account. Hayes later told Gardaí that the blows from the stick failed to render the widow unconscious – they only seemed to wound the frail woman.

Hayes decided on more drastic action. He remembered a piece of heavy kitchen worktop that was lying in his house. He grabbed the heavy piece of timber and struck her twice on the head. The widow – who was tied up with electrical cord and a dog lead – immediately fell to the ground, apparently knocked unconscious. Hayes then went and got the bank cards and prepared to start withdrawing money from her account.

Hayes later told Gardaí that when he checked on the widow, she was making a noise, which he thought sounded like snoring. Despite the freezing cold weather, he left her lying on the ground tied to the chair overnight. When he checked on her the next day, she had died. It was a tragic end to a life filled with kindness and devotion to others. One of the most distressing aspects of the entire case for the Corcoran family was imagining the abject terror and pain of Ann's last few hours alive.

In a grim sequence of events, Hayes left the widow where she had died for a further twenty-four hours while he figured out a plan for what to do next. The court later heard that while Hayes had admitted striking the widow repeatedly over the head in a bid to knock her out, he had never properly explained how the sixty-year-old had suffered bruising to her eyes and cuts to the inside of her mouth. These were detected during a painstaking post mortem examination conducted following the recovery of Ann's body by Gardaí.

Hayes himself cut a somewhat pathetic figure in court. When a video recording of his confession to Gardaí was played for the jury on the sixth day of his Dublin murder trial, Hayes broke down and quietly began sobbing. The tape revealed the detailed planning that had gone into the robbery and just how desperate he was to get cash. 'As she [Ann] was going for the front door I caught her from behind and asked for money. I just put my hand around her neck – [at first] she tried to struggle a small bit. After about ten minutes she wasn't saying anything. She said she hadn't any money, that it was all in the bank. So I told her I would take her away until I had some [money]. She said she would go to the bank with me and get it out. She only wanted to get away. I thought it was only a ploy to get out to the open and I wasn't going to fall for that. I tied her hands with washing line cord.'

Having put the terrified woman in the boot of her own car, Hayes decided to exert maximum psychological pressure in a bid to get the information he needed. 'I stopped [the car] in a few places and asked her again.' Despite her obvious terror, Ann Corcoran refused to cooperate with her abductor. Only then did Hayes decide that the only option was to take her back to his Clancool Terrace home where he could get the PIN information he needed.

Incredibly, by the time he arrived at his home, the widow had managed to free herself and had partially climbed through to the back seat of her car. 'I just pulled her out really – with my hand kind of around her mouth so that she wouldn't say anything. I told her she would have to stay here until I got some [money]. So after about half an hour she gave [me] the number. She [said she] had the card back in her house. So I wanted to knock her out. I hit her with a board and it didn't take any affect. So then I hit her with the other board – it was a bit heavier.'

In the video interview, Hayes also described how he discovered that the widow had died overnight. 'She was not breathing and I saw an awful lot of blood on the ground. So I went back downstairs for about an hour and sat back down. I did not know what to do at that stage. I never meant to do it,' he told detectives. Hayes needed time to think – but it still did not stop him carrying on with his normal interests. While Ann Corcoran lay dead in his home, Hayes attended the weekly meeting of his camera club and even went for a few drinks afterwards.

What most horrified everyone were the awful circumstances in which Ann died. The house-proud widow died in Hayes' Clancool Terrace home, which was so untidy and rubbish-strewn that veteran detectives were shocked at what they discovered. Hayes' home was so packed with rubbish, decorating debris and old collectable magazines ranging from part-works to crime series that, in parts, it was difficult even to physically move around. The house had a rodent infestation problem.

It took Gardaí twenty-four hours just to empty Hayes' home of rubbish before they could begin their meticulous forensic examination of the scene where the widow died. At one point, the body of a dead rodent was discovered in the house. In contrast, Ann Corcoran's house was described by one neighbour as perennially 'like a new pin', with the widow working hard to ensure both her home and garden were always in immaculate condition.

The reasons for Hayes' determination to get cash quickly became apparent. He was heavily in debt – he owed €12,000 to a west Cork credit union, he had yet to pay a shop for an expensive camera that he had set his heart on and he did not even have the cash to get his old Fiat Scudo van repaired. He had not made mortgage payments on his Clancool Terrace home in almost two years. He acknowledged in later Garda interviews that his debts and financial situation were giving him 'a lot of sleepless nights'. But Hayes' financial problems did not seem to impact on his social life.

Hayes had an expensive taste for travel. His long-term girlfriend was planning to go on a skiing holiday to Austria and he was determined to accompany her. Over the previous few years, Hayes had also travelled to Australia and even Israel – holidays that were expensive by any standards. Yet work remained intermittent for him and even at the peak of the Celtic Tiger years, Hayes was always struggling to make ends meet. Those who knew him later admitted that he was always more interested in the photographic projects going on with the camera club of which he was a member than getting painting or decorating work for his business.

'In January 2009, work was quiet,' Hayes had explained to his trial. 'I had put off paying some of the bigger bills thinking that something might come around the corner.' But, with nothing in sight, Hayes was becoming desperate. He needed cash to meet bills that were now pressing in upon him – and he wanted to maintain his social life. Hayes decided that his best option for raising cash was to steal it. His preference was not to target a business or an individual who might fight back. No, he would target the vulnerable – someone he could terrify easily.

'I thought I'd go to some place and rob it,' he said. Hayes' preference was now to target an older woman, living alone. Ann Corcoran had simply been the first target to come to mind. What Ann and many other people in the tightly knit west Cork community did not realise was that Oliver Hayes had targeted older women for robberies before, but none had ever gone this far.

Hayes now realised he had to dispose of Ann Corcoran's body. He decided to destroy any evidence that might link him to the widow's death. He had been fascinated by crime magazines and so knew just how important forensic and technical evidence was. He also knew from his reading just how capable and thorough modern crime scene investigators are. So he brought Ann's body to Kilmore Woods, an isolated tract of forestry between Ballinspittle and Garretstown. Hayes knew the area well from his countryside walks and hoped that the body might never be found in such an isolated spot. Poignantly, Kilmore Woods was located off a road that Ann Corcoran would have travelled many times during her life, little realising it would prove her temporary resting place after her murder. Hayes dug a shallow grave and then, after soaking the body in petrol, set it alight. When the flames had died down, he covered the grave with clippings, twigs and then some stones. Ann Corcoran's body was eventually recovered by Gardaí from Kilmore Woods on 6 February, almost two weeks after she had disappeared.

One of the most disturbing elements of the case was that Hayes – after bludgeoning the frail widow to death – had travelled back out to her house to ensure that her dogs were properly fed and had access to fresh water. His concern for the pets of the woman he had just killed appeared both genuine and sincere. 'I am kind to animals,' Hayes later explained to shocked detectives. The painter then became upset when he considered the suffering of the dogs locked alone inside Ann Corcoran's house while he was overseas on the holiday funded by his theft. He insisted to Gardaí, apparently trying to persuade them of his sincere love for animals, that he had left enough food out for the dogs while he was in Austria to ensure they would not starve to death or die of dehydration.

Hayes eventually used Ann Corcoran's ATM card to make five withdrawals from her account to a total of €3,000. This was the cash that helped pay for his Austrian skiing break. His girlfriend – whom he had been dating for almost ten years – had absolutely no inkling as to where Hayes had obtained the money. Despite the fact that they had been dating for almost a decade, the woman had never been to Hayes' Clancool Terrace home.

In getting cash from Ann Corcoran's bank accounts, Hayes had carefully tried to disguise his appearance to avoid identification, realising that CCTV security cameras were installed near the ATMs and on the streets he would have to use. The CCTV cameras did in fact record an individual making the withdrawals and Hayes had not disguised his appearance carefully enough for eagle-eyed Gardaí.

Detectives quickly realised that whoever had made the withdrawals from Ann Corcoran's bank account after the widow had vanished was most likely responsible for her disappearance and death. The CCTV footage immediately became the central element of the Garda probe and officers from throughout the west Cork division were shown the footage to see if anyone recognised the disguised individual trying to avoid the cameras while making withdrawals from Ann Corcoran's accounts.

One officer studied the footage and noticed something unusual. The man walking away from the ATM machine had a distinctive gait, almost a cross between a limp and a roll of his hips. It was a gait that was as unusual as it was distinctive. The Garda knew a man who had that type of walk: Oliver Hayes. Another detective focused on a different element of the CCTV footage. It was the type of hat worn by the man. The hat was clearly being used to try to cover the man's face from the camera. But the Garda believed the hat was similar to a cap that Oliver Hayes had bought while on holiday in Israel several years beforehand. A closer analysis revealed it was almost certainly the same hat.

In the fortnight after Ann Corcoran disappeared, Gardaí mounted one of the biggest search operations in Irish history. Detectives knew they had to find the widow's body, which would, in turn, lead them to her killer. Without the body, they did not have a crime scene and without that a court conviction would be problematic. The Garda appeal for help with their search operation resulted in a tidal wave of volunteers coming forward. Gardaí were assisted by Defence Forces personnel, Civil Defence, Irish Coastguard, Coastal Rescue as well as the Air Corps. West Cork groups ranging from hill-walking clubs to the Irish Farmers' Association

(IFA) came forward to offer assistance. Eventually, up to 400 people a day were combing forests, rivers, ditches, glens and scrubland around Bandon. Many defied atrocious weather conditions, including rain, snow, ice and frost.

But the CCTV footage and its analysis meant the investigation was now focused very closely on Oliver Hayes. Detectives were forced to move quickly when one tabloid newspaper revealed what a critical role the CCTV footage was now playing in the investigation. Oliver Hayes was arrested on Thursday 5 February 2009 and, after several hours of questioning, provided crucial information to detectives.

That evening, Gardaí switched the focus of their search operation to Kilmore Woods. Search teams were given a specific area to examine, about 100 metres from the roadway and not far from a rutted forestry track. The following day, Friday 6 February 2009, Gardaí confirmed that a body had been recovered. It was Ann Corcoran. However, it would be almost twenty-four hours before the widow's charred body could be moved because of the need to conduct an exhaustive technical examination of the area. Gardaí had, by now, also sealed off Oliver Hayes' home at Clancool Terrace.

When he was first charged with the widow's disappearance, Hayes simply told Gardaí: 'I am sorry for what happened – I never meant for her to die.' West Cork locals were not so understanding. Hayes was brought before a special sitting of Bandon District Court that same Friday evening and was charged with the false imprisonment of Ann Corcoran. Outside the courthouse, an angry crowd of 300 people had gathered – many of whom had spent the previous three weeks searching the local countryside for the widow.

Locals were relieved that the widow's body had been found and that Gardaí had made an arrest. But as word spread that the man arrested was a local, the public reaction was one of disbelieving fury.

The mood was ugly as Gardaí escorting Hayes arrived at the courthouse. As officers accompanied him into the building, they were jostled by the crowd. Abuse was shouted at the 49-year-old who entered the court premises with his head fully covered. Hayes' knees were actually shaking as he was rushed through the crowd by a phalanx of uniformed Gardaí. One angry man slapped the side of a squad car carrying the defendant away from the brief court hearing as Hayes was remanded in custody by Judge James McNulty. 'Take off the hood, you tramp,' one member of the public roared as Hayes kept his head lowered in the squad car. Others joined in the cacophony of abuse with jeers to Hayes of 'lousy bastard' and 'rot in hell'. At one point, a bottle was thrown from the crowd.

The Central Criminal Court was later told that Hayes had a total of eight previous convictions, two of which involved the robbery of elderly woman in the west Cork area. Pointedly, Hayes had never received a custodial sentence before receiving a mandatory life term for Ann Corcoran's murder.

One of his previous convictions included the burglary of an 84-year-old woman's home where Hayes turned off her ESB supply so that he could better conduct the robbery of her home in darkness. He eventually stole £3,000 and some jewellery. The woman later fell out of bed in the darkness. While she was uninjured in the incident, she was upset by the ordeal. She died some four months later. Hayes also tried to rob a woman in her late fifties after confronting her at her home with a knife. However, she had the presence of mind to scream loudly and a neighbour was alerted. As the neighbour rushed to her aid, Hayes then fled the scene only to be detained later by Gardaí. Tragically, Ann Corcoran would not prove to be that lucky.

5

Manuela Riedo

'Death of an Angel'

To the uninformed, they were merely a couple of European tourists enjoying a typical autumn city break in Galway. Hans-Pieter and Arlette Riedo smiled at the crowds that waved kindly to them and paused to enjoy the panoramic views out over Galway Bay. It was a blustery October day in Galway and the wind had whipped the tops of the waves into white foam as they crashed onto the rocks by the shore at Salthill. The day was dry and clear and the Connemara coast was visible sweeping into the distance.

But Hans-Pieter and Arlette were not just any ordinary European couple enjoying an Irish break. The Swiss couple had lost the most precious thing in their lives in this very city – their only child, Mauela (seventeen) – and they were in Ireland to participate in a moving ceremony of remembrance.

It was fitting that the Swiss couple were joined by Michael and Marie Phelan from Roscrea, County Tipperary. The two couples silently linked arms as they stood by the Salthill strand and watched as dozens of balloons were set free in a coordinated release. Each balloon was released by a Galway person appalled at the violent crimes that had claimed lives within their community. Most were there because they were particularly heartsick at what the Swiss couple had endured following the brutal murder of their only child two years previous.

Michael and Marie stood shoulder to shoulder beside Hans-Pieter and Arlette because their own son, Colm (twenty-six), died after an attack involving the very same man who had killed Manuela. It was a link that no parent could forget. Colm had been attending a stag party in Galway with some friends in 1996. He ended up in Eyre Square and was waiting patiently for a taxi when, without provocation, he and his friends were attacked by a gang of local youngsters. One of the men was Gerald Barry (twenty-nine). In the course of the fight, Colm sustained fatal injuries. It remains unclear whether the head injuries Colm suffered were from a kick to the head or a blow from a bottle. Barry was only sixteen at the time and was subsequently convicted of violent disorder. He was jailed for five years, yet ultimately served just two.

The balloons – on release – were instantly whipped up into the grey-and-blue sky over Galway. The crowd watched silently as the tiny dots of colour zipped erratically over the bay before finally vanishing into the misty distance. It was a fitting gesture of remembrance because Manuela's funeral had been marked by a similar balloon release, symbolic of spirits being set free on the wind.

Hans-Pieter, Arlette, Michael and Marie embraced as tears streaked their windswept cheeks and memories of loved ones lost came flooding back. The awful reality is that both had lost something special, something irreplaceable in a city that prides itself as an artistic hub and one of Europe's safest places to live. Manuela and Colm had both gone to Galway for events that should have been joyous. Yet both ended up coming home in coffins.

The pain was certainly eased by the tidal wave of emotional support shown for both families by the ordinary people of Galway. Locals were sickened and appalled that the families should have endured such pain in their city – and were determined that the gratuitous, cruel acts of violence should not be seen to be typical of their proud city. That fact was borne out by the turnout for the memorial and the high-profile endorsements of the event by virtually every political, cultural, religious and business group in Galway.

The Riedos and Phelans had been guests of honour in the Salthill Hotel, which had agreed to host a special memorial concert for the victims of violent crime. The concert was specifically dedicated to the memory of Manuela and the star-studded line-up underlined just how much her murder had shocked the local community. Artists who had immediately agreed to support the event included Sharon Shannon, Marc Roberts, the Mulkerrin Brothers, Lucia Evans and Frank Naughton. The event, needless to say, proved a sell-out success. Sharon Shannon said the young Swiss girl's killing had had a traumatic impact on a community unused to such violence. 'Manuela is in my mind a lot. It's so terrible what happened to her and I think it's very important for the people of Galway to do something to honour her memory and help other victims. I think it is also important to show support for her parents and that she is not forgotten,' she said.

The proceeds of the event would go towards a new charity – the Manuela Riedo Foundation – which would now try and offer help and support to the victims of rape throughout Europe. The charity was set up by Brendan McGuinness, an Irish businessman who owns a pub in Basel in Switzerland. It meant a lot to Hans-Pieter and Arlette that, while their daughter was no longer with them, her name would at least be remembered. Fiona Neary of the Rape Crisis Network said that such positive developments are hugely important for victims' families. 'Obviously, the Riedos are particularly interested in projects that support victims of sexual violence and projects around education and prevention to avoid crimes like this in the future,' she explained.

Inevitably, despite the warmth of their welcome to Galway, Hans-Pieter admitted that the city would always hold mixed emotions for him. 'We were nervous coming back to Galway, but it is getting a little easier each time. We are very grateful to the organisers and the people of Galway for staging this event,' he said. The visit was no easier for the Phelans – with Michael and Marie having steadfastly avoided Galway in the years since their son's tragic death. They had only decided to attend the special concert after receiving a letter from

Hans-Pieter and Arlette asking them to go. Poignantly, both families had found support and understanding together after the realisation that they had both lost their loved ones because of the brutal actions of the same man.

'We are very pleased to support this special event. It is our first time back and it hasn't been easy. But Mr and Mrs Riedo have written to us and we have been in touch. We are very pleased to meet them here in Galway,' Michael said. Both couples now found solidarity and strength in each other's company. But some memories of Galway are not easy to deal with.

'The first time we were here it was very difficult to go down to the crime scene. As we come back frequently, it gets easier each time,' Hans-Pieter, speaking through an interpreter, explained. 'We now have so many friends in Galway it obviously helps us through the process.' The couple are now readily known in the city and, as they walk around the streets during their regular visits, they are warmly greeted by locals, some of whom do not personally know the Riedos but want to share a kind word or simply wish them well.

The Riedos received a standing ovation from a sell-out crowd of more than 1,200 at the Salthill Hotel in an emotionally charged opening to the concert. For Hans-Pieter and Arlette it was almost too much to cope with – that so many people shared their pain at Manuela's loss, so desperately wanted to help ease the burden of their suffering. 'Thank you so much for coming. You make it easier for us. You have given me hope for the future,' Hans-Pieter said to the crowd in halting English. His brief address earned another standing ovation.

The tragedy for both the Riedos and the Phelans is

that their loved ones could not have met a more dangerous individual on their separate social outings than Gerald Barry. In hindsight, the warning signs were all too evident that Barry posed a serious threat to Galway society. Born in Mervue in 1980, a sprawling suburb of Galway city, Barry's life was chaotic virtually from the start. One of nine children, his mother was left to care alone for her five boys and four girls when her husband moved out of the family home. A long-distance truck driver by profession, he never subsequently moved back – and the woman was left to cope with nine youngsters on meager resources.

She struggled to manage and a growing personal alcohol problem only made matters worse. In the end, the children were basically left free to roam the streets – and by the time he was in his early teens Gerald Barry was already virtually out of control. He made the sprawling housing estate of Rahoon his home and quickly became involved in drugs and cider parties. Alcohol became a dominant feature of Gerald Barry's life. He quickly became known – and feared – throughout Rahoon and Galway for his propensity for violence and his cruelty.

It was not long before he came to Garda attention and, after ignoring repeated warnings, was sent to juvenile detention centres including Trinity House and St Patrick's Institution, both in County Dublin. Far from helping calm Gerald Barry down, the institutions merely exacerbated his violent personality. His crimes soon escalated from the petty to the increasingly violent. Over time he built up a formidable list of convictions before Galway District Court ranging from robbery, drunk and disorderly, drug possession and Road Traffic Act (RTA) breaches.

Tellingly, Gerald Barry was only sixteen when he became involved in the Eyre Square brawl that cost Colm Phelan his life in July 1996. Despite his years, the indications were that Barry was one of the main instigators of the unprovoked attack. Other members of the gang pleaded guilty to violent disorder but Barry insisted on contesting the charge. On conviction, he was jailed for five years. He showed little sign of remorse.

Once released from custody, his behaviour became even more violent and uncontrolled. In one incident, he attacked an elderly man in his own home during a robbery that spiralled out of control. Such were the horrific injuries sustained by the pensioner that he was left completely blind. Barry went back to prison for two years. But the violence was also spilling over into his personal life. Despite the fact he was notorious in Galway as an aggressive, unpredictable individual given to violent outbursts, a young Galway woman still managed to get entangled in a relationship with Barry.

It was a relationship that was doomed from the start. The woman suffered beatings, threats, jealousy, alcohol-fuelled rages and emotional chaos. She became pregnant by Barry but, even after she gave birth to a healthy baby, the beatings and violence continued. In 2004, fearful for her own safety and that of her baby, she left Barry. Gardaí at the time were concerned for her and acknowledged that the woman had endured frightful abuse at Barry's hands. Yet Barry was having none of it. He would follow the woman in the street and keep vigil outside her new accommodation. He steadfastly refused to let go of the relationship.

In 2005, he managed to break into the woman's home

and, despite the fact the baby was in the house, subjected her to a terrifying assault. The woman was left traumatised but reported the incident to Gardaí and successfully secured a protection order. Yet Gerald Barry's orgy of violence was about to reach its crescendo – and, in the space of just seven weeks, it would claim two more victims, one to rape and murder and the other to a brutal, multiple rape.

On 16 August 2007, Gerald Barry again called to his former partner's home. She refused him admission and tried to warn him off, threatening to alert the Gardaí. But he still tried to force his way into the house, which provoked a struggle and then a vicious fight. The woman was assaulted and Barry fled the scene on foot before Gardaí could arrive. The traumatised woman later reported the incident to the Gardaí and officers went looking for Barry.

But Barry – infuriated and determined to indulge his animal passions – went looking for another victim. He didn't have to look far. As he approached the Mervue estate, he spotted a young woman walking in the distance. It turned out to be a 21-year-old French student who was returning to her lodgings having spent the evening in Galway city centre. She had attended a special traditional music session and had parted company from her university friends earlier and was walking home alone.

Barry stalked her and chose his moment near St James' GAA grounds. He ran up behind the woman, grabbed her by the hair, held a knife to her throat and warned her not to scream. He dragged her off the pathway and into a dark corner of the grounds where he partially tore off her clothing and anally raped her. Throughout the rape, he held a knife to her throat and warned her to be quiet. Barry then demanded that the woman perform oral sex on him and he promised he would let her go unharmed if she complied with his instructions. But once the terrified woman had done as he had ordered, he violently raped her twice more. Barry then fled leaving the sobbing, bleeding woman lying on the ground. In an animalistic aside, Barry spotted that the young woman had suffered an internal injury after the third rape and told her: 'Hey, you're bleeding – great!'

The French woman was so traumatised that when she finally managed to get to Galway hospital she could not explain what had just happened to her. Unable to verbally outline the bestial attack she had suffered, she was forced to write on a piece of paper for doctors: 'I was raped.' Only then were Gardaí informed.

Events subsequently moved quickly. Barry's ex-partner made a formal complaint to Gardaí about the fresh assault she had suffered at his hands. Detectives became aware of the woman's statement and were immediately suspicious of the fact that Gerald Barry was in the vicinity where the rape of the French woman had occurred at roughly the same time. When Barry was finally located, he was brought to the Garda Station for questioning. He initially insisted that he went straight home after the confrontation with his ex-girlfriend – but eagle-eyed detectives realised that the clothes still worn by Barry precisely matched the description given by the terrorised young student of the man who had raped her.

Barry was charged on 18 August before Galway District Court with an assault against his former partner. But the rape investigation was still ongoing and a file would have to be sent to the DPP before a charge could be considered. The process was slowed by the need to await the results of key forensic tests including DNA analysis. Gardaí objected to Barry being released on bail but were unable to indicate that he would likely be charged in relation to the attack on the French student. Despite the Garda request for a remand in custody, Barry was granted bail by the judge. Seven weeks later, Gerald Barry would kill Manuela Riedo in an attack that was a near mirror-image of the rape of the French student.

In a quirk of the legal system, Manuela's murder trial was staged before the rape case of the French student. But the French woman's victim impact statement in 2009 underlined just how dangerous and predatory Barry was. The woman – who is still traumatised by the attack – said she is now surprised she ever survived Barry's assault. 'When I am thinking of what had happened, I do not understand why I am breathing right now. Why am I not dead? Why did that man leave me, go and decide that I was allowed to live? Many questions, far fewer answers that will never come,' she said.

The young woman said that her confidence was shattered by the attack and that she was plagued by nightmares for months after the rape. Even today, she is nervous and uncomfortable when left alone around men. '[I am afraid] when a man is walking behind me or someone touches my back, my neck or my hair. It is my body and I cannot permit anyone else to touch me or to get too close to me without getting concerned.

'He [Barry] is not human or a man. He is a liar, a murderer, a rapist and he is one of a crazy, inconceivable breed. He is a human predator – and he has to be punished for what he did. [His life] is nothing but disgusting, bad actions against other people. How can he sleep at night? Be living, breathing, walking, laughing, and listening to music?' The woman added that every time she reads about the attack on her, the terrible memories of that night come flooding back. 'It happened to me and not to them [reporters]. They talk of it as if it was an everyday life story. I try to forget about this but they bring me back to that day. The newspapers are not conscious of the harm caused by such articles.'

In hindsight, it is nothing short of incredible that the young French woman survived the attack. But Manuela Riedo would not be so fortunate. The Swiss teen would not live through her encounter with Gerald Barry. The seventeen-year-old had only arrived in Ireland on 5 October 2007 as part of an English language course. It was the Swiss teen's first ever visit overseas without her parents – and they specifically chose Galway over a similar trip to London because they thought Ireland would be safer for their only daughter than the British capital.

Manuela was thrilled at the prospect of the trip and had been talking for weeks beforehand with her Bern schoolfriends about it. She had separated from her fellow students in Galway on the evening of October 8 – and had arranged to meet up with them in the city where they hoped to go and listen to some traditional music. Manuela left her lodgings and headed into the city – but decided to walk alone. Fatefully, she also decided to go along a walkway, which ran beside the railway tracks from Renmore to Galway city. Locals dubbed the walkway 'The Line' but it was isolated and generally avoided at night-time by woman walking alone.

The foreign language students had been told to stay together and not to use 'The Line'.

Tierneys of Renmore Park, Galway, were Manuela's host family during her stay. Martin Tierney later told a Galway coroner's inquest that he had advised the Swiss teen not to use 'The Line' that evening as a shortcut because he would not himself walk the route alone at night. It was Mr Tierney who first raised the alarm when Manuela's breakfast place setting was untouched the following morning – and, after he contacted the language school officials, raised the alarm when no one knew where Manuela was.

Gerald Barry's initial story to Gardaí was that he met Manuela during her walk and she asked him the time. He claimed they struck up a conversation, liked each other's company and then agreed to have consensual sex. He insisted that Manuela's death was an accident, which occurred as he tried to persuade her not to go into town and stay with him. Barry added that he only took items belonging to Manuela, including her camera, when he spotted them after they had accidentally fallen out of her bag. It was a hare-brained story that few gave any credence to.

The grim reality is that the final moments of the Swiss teen's life must have been agonising. When her body was eventually found, it was semi-naked and lying on waste ground at Lough Atalia, just off 'The Line'. Manuela was found by Galway artist Sam Beardon as he was taking a morning walk at Lough Atalia. A jacket had been placed over her face and held down by a stone. A post mortem examination revealed that Manuela had died from manual strangulation. State Pathologist Dr Marie Cassidy found that the body had head and neck injuries and a gaping wound to the left groin. Shockingly, the teen had injuries to the genital area. The pathologist surmised that the genital injuries may have been caused by a rough object being forced against her vagina. As asphyxial signs were present, Prof. Cassidy ruled that Manuela's death was due to neck compression.

Some of the teen's possessions were missing and, in almost callous fashion, a condom was found dangling from a nearby bush. Gardaí carefully recovered the item and sent it for full genetic-fingerprinting analysis. It was found to contain Gerald Barry's DNA. Some of Manuela's possessions, including a camera and a mobile phone, were later recovered by Gardaí from Barry's home.

Hans-Pieter and Arlette wanted to come to Ireland to escort their daughter's body back home to Bern in Switzerland but they simply were not able. The emotions surrounding the loss of their only child were too great. Privately, the couple vowed to travel to Galway someday and lay a single rose at the spot where their beloved daughter died. Manuela's funeral service on 19 October offered little consolation. The glorious sunshine of the Swiss autumn afternoon and the welcome news that Galway Gardaí had made an arrest in their murder probe could not mask the fact they were saying their final farewell to the child they had raised, nurtured and for whom they had harboured such great hopes. Back in Galway, 1,000 people had packed into Renmore Parish Church the evening before Manuela's Swiss funeral for a special service as a gesture of support and solidarity.

In Switzerland, there was no consoling Manuela's parents. Neighbours, friends and extended family did their best to comfort the distressed couple but even they were almost too overcome by the sheer awfulness of Manuela's brutal death. All family, friends and neighbours could do was weep silently alongside Hans-Pieter and Arlette. Manuela's teenage friends in Hinterkappelen and Wohlen, adjoining villages on the outskirts of Bern, were joined by her schoolmates who arrived at the service carrying single stemmed roses as a tribute to their lost friend.

In a gesture aimed at underlining the horror of the Irish nation at the murder, both the government and Galway authorities were represented at the service. Ireland's Ambassador to Switzerland, James Sharkey, personally expressed the nation's sorrow to Hans-Pieter and Arlette. All of Ireland mourned with them, the Ambassador said. 'In this community and in Fribourg [where Manuela went to school] there is a sense of complete distress that someone so young and so beautiful has been taken away,' Ambassador Sharkey explained.

The Mayor of Galway, Cllr Tom Costello, had asked to visit the school at Fribourg that had supplied so many of the group with which Manuela had travelled to Ireland. Brian McDonald reported in the *Irish Independent* that Cllr Costello told the students that the killing had had the same impact on the Irish community as it had on their own Swiss community. Galway shared their hurt, their horror and their heartache over what had happened. He also presented Manuela's parents with a formal message of sympathy from the city of Galway.

The efforts of the Irish authorities in trying to assuage the grief of the Riedo family were acknowledged with appreciation by the Swiss community. The Mayor of Wohlen, Cllr Christian Muller, said that while the area was numbed with sadness at Manuela's death, the kindness of the Irish people and authorities over the tragedy had been noted. 'We know that what happened was the action of one man and not the Irish people.'

The funeral service itself at the Reformed Protestant Church in Wohlen was as touching as it was beautiful. Manuela's coffin was covered in flowers, mostly roses. The only other adornment was a small angel. The parish leader, Barbara Kuckelmann, led the service and said everyone had found it very moving that a group from Galway had travelled all the way to be with the Swiss community at such a difficult time. Ms Kuckelmann said over the past week she had heard Manuela described as 'a wonderful, unique young woman' who was kind and gentle towards others.

She particularly noted Manuela's love of angels and her ardent desire to help others. The preacher said that she had no doubt that Manuela had now joined the angels who had so captivated her in life. 'Let her now light up our hearts so we can avoid the darkness,' Ms Kuckelmann told the congregation. At the specific request of Hans-Pieter and Arlette, a piece of music was played during the ceremony which contained the moving line: 'If there were angels on earth, you would be one, for sure.' The other songs played involved some of Manuela's favourite music and, in turn, reflected her tender years. There was James Blunt's '1973', Leonard Cohen's 'Hallelujah', 'Memories' from the hit musical *Cats* and a particular Swiss pop hit, 'Eternal Love'.

As the funeral service commenced, a Swiss flag was

lowered to half-mast over Galway's City Hall in a gesture of cross-community solidarity and mourning. Back in Wohlen, fourteen of Manuela's closest friends from her dance troupe put on a special tribute to their lost friend – and, as the piece concluded, several of the teens collapsed in tears and had to support each other back to the church pews. Another friend penned a special tribute which was read out at the conclusion of the ceremony. It read: 'The flowers have lost their scent, the sun has lost its warmth, everything is still. You cheered us up and filled our classroom with love and warmth, we will never forget you.'

As the service concluded and mourners left the church, each was handed a coloured balloon. The mourners then gathered in a green, open space outside the church. A lone drummer began a slow drum roll and the balloons were released by each of the mourners, almost immediately swept away into the Swiss sky.

Hans-Pieter and Arlette embraced, struggled to control their emotions and turned to the waiting crowd. In a spontaneous address in German, Manuela's father thanked everyone for the support he and his wife had received at such a traumatic time. He was aware that everyone stood with them and he hoped that the funeral service helped them to come to terms with what had happened. Arlette Riedo added that she would not forget Ireland and vowed one day to visit the place where her daughter spent her final hours. In January 2008, Arlette would fulfill her vow to Manuela. In the funeral crowd, the Irish delegation was deeply touched by the Riedo family's generosity of spirit.

Back in Ireland, Gardaí had prepared a powerful case

against Gerald Barry. But, despite the overwhelming evidence against him, Barry still chose to contest the murder charge. After a seven-day Central Criminal Court trial in 2008, he was unanimously convicted by the jury. The six men and six women of the jury convicted Barry of the Manuela's murder after taking just two hours and thirty-eight minutes to reach their verdict. In the wake of the verdict and sentencing, senior Gardaí admitted that Galway was now a safer place with Gerald Barry behind bars for years to come.

The trial was an unmitigated nightmare for Hans-Pieter and Arlette Riedo who were forced to listen not only to the appalling manner in which their daughter died but also to Barry's snide, almost casual claims, which made up his version of how the pretty Swiss teen had died. What made matters all the more difficult is that the Riedos were forced to follow proceedings with the help of an interpreter.

When Hans-Pieter's victim impact statement was read out in court before Barry was handed the mandatory life sentence for murder, the magnitude of his brutal crime was laid bare. In graphic terms, the Swiss father outlined how Barry had robbed them of every single thing they held precious in life – and how he had robbed the world of a teenager who simply wanted to make a difference.

'We cannot really put into words what the death of our beloved daughter Manuela has taken away from us. You [Barry] have robbed Manuela of sixty to seventy years of her life and taken the future away from us, her parents. I will never lead my daughter as a bride to the altar and my wife will never knit baby clothes for her grandchild. We won't have anyone to look after us when we are old,' he said.

'When Manuela was born on 5 November 1989, a new challenge began for us as her parents. We were able then to give this tiny, helpless, beautiful child everything that parents should give – we gave love, friendship, honesty, warmth, security and much more. We were able to watch Manuela grow up from a little baby to a unique, wonderful person. With her special manner she was loved and respected by everyone. She was a good friend, a good student – she was our pride and joy. We were so happy to have such a daughter – these wonderful memories are all that is left for us,' he added.

'Manuela knew exactly what she wanted to do in the future. She had big career plans. She wanted to go to the United States and attend a language school and then attend a hotel management school back in Switzerland. Her dream was to become a tour guide so as to get to know different countries, their culture and people in her life.

'Already in her childhood she would approach other people and she was especially open to people with problems. During her school years, for example, there was a physically handicapped girl in her class. Manuela was the only one in the class who always included that girl in all her activities. She didn't have any fears of contact with others. As an only child she was able to share with others from an early age. Sometimes she shared so much of what she had with others that she ended up with nothing herself. But it was more important for her to make others happy.

'Already at the age of fourteen it was clear to her that when she began to earn her own money, she would support a foster child through the World Vision [charity]. In the time shortly before her death, she wrote a paper for the vocational school she was attending about a project in Nicaragua. One week before her trip to Ireland, she was able to complete that project and she was proud to be able to hand it in. She had worked for hours on that project because it had always been important to her to do everything well and as perfectly as possible. After her death, her teacher told us that she had received a very good mark on the project.'

Hans-Pieter and Arlette knew that Manuela needed her own space given that she was almost eighteen – and her trip to Ireland was part of that growth experience. They judged that if the trip to Ireland went well, Manuela would have proved herself ready for longer-haul trips. The couple had heard only positive stories about Ireland and they said they had no worries about sending their only child to Galway. 'We had heard only good things about Ireland and thus we had no misgivings about sending her to this beautiful country,' he said. The Riedos only concern was that Manuela would not get too homesick for her parents and her beloved home at Hinterkappelen.

'Manuela was the centre of our life and our sunshine. We are so proud of her. She was always a polite, courteous, attentive and cheerful girl who was loved by everyone. There are no words to describe adequately her wonderful character and disposition. You should have known her. Then it would be clear to you immediately what we mean. Anyone who knew her could not easily forget her. She was loved by her fellow students, both boys and girls, and had a special place in the hearts of many people,' Hans-Pieter added. 'Manuela was crazy about dancing. She was in a dance group for hip-hop and for jazz. Her teacher told us that Manuela always brought a cheerful and buoyant atmosphere with her to the dance studio and that everyone felt better when she was there. When she wasn't there she was missed by everyone. Now she will be missed by everyone forever.'

The tragedy of her murder in Galway was underlined by just how protective Hans-Pieter and Arlette were of their daughter back home in Switzerland. 'We always looked out for Manuela very carefully. As her father, I often drove her out with the car at night to pick her up so that she would arrive safely back home. No way was too long for me to bring her back. We have lost our angel but we have gotten to know many fine people now [in Ireland]. Manuela loved angels and we have brought three angels with us . . .

'Here in Dublin we have seen and heard the other side. People have told us everything that we wanted to know. So now Manuela's soul can finally rest in peace and we can let our angel fly to God, our Lord in Heaven. Manuela, rest in peace – you will remain forever in our hearts.' Back in the public gallery, Hans-Pieter and Arlette embraced, tears streaming down both their faces.

Gerald Barry received a life sentence for the murder of Manuela Riedo – and, the next year (2009), received two further life sentences for the brutal rape of the young French student. The two trial judges – Mr Justice Barry White (Riedo) and Mr Justice Paul Carney (French student) – were in total agreement about the sentences required for Barry's crimes.

Mr Justice White effectively reflected the mood of the nation when he directly addressed a heartbroken Hans-Pieter and Arlette in the Central Criminal Court. 'In expressing my sympathies I have no doubt I am also expressing the sympathies of every right-minded citizen in the country – [and I hope] they can find it in their hearts to forgive the Irish nation,' he declared.

Mr Justice Carney went even further, warning that Barry – unlike other sentenced criminals – did not necessarily deserve any 'tunnel of light' at the end of his sentence. Barry, perhaps true to form, showed little or no emotion at the judge's comments. His only reaction was to cock his head and stare at the judge as he made his sentencing comments – a move interpreted by the *Sunday Independent* as a gesture of defiance. Barry demonstrated no personal remorse to the families of his Swiss and French victims.

Mr Justice Carney bluntly described Barry's rape of the young French woman as 'an outrage' – and said that there was little doubt that Barry had the 'propensity to kill or rape and is highly likely to do so again if given the opportunity'. In a comment that will remain on the trial record which will be studied at a future date by the Parole Board, Mr Justice Carney said that not all prisoners are necessarily entitled to the 'tunnel of hope' offered by sentence reduction. 'This is a concept built in gentler times before the scourge of drugs made some people mindless, wholly irrational and evil,' he warned.

The sad reality is that Gerald Barry's criminal career also raised significant issues for the Irish justice system even before it was finally brought to a halt by the Central Criminal Court. Most of all, the 'what ifs' in the handling of Barry by the judicial system over the years have caused the greatest concern. Barry had been convicted of malicious damage and received an eighteen-month sentence, which, if it had been served in its entirety, would have meant he would not have been on the streets of Galway to attack Colm Phelan in 1996. Equally, had Barry been remanded in custody by the District Court – as Gardaí clearly wanted in August 2007 – he would have been behind bars and not free to confront Manuela Riedo fatally at Lough Atalia.

Today, Hans-Pieter and Arlette are rebuilding their lives back in Hinterkappelen. They have made new friends in Galway and visit Ireland at least once every year. When they arrive in Galway, they are treated as long-lost friends and locals cannot seem to do enough for the Swiss couple. At Renmore, the spot where Manuela died is now marked by a little shrine, lovingly maintained by local people. There are plans in Galway to erect a permanent stone memorial to the angel whose life was so tragically cut short.

The Manuela Riedo Foundation continues to raise money for the support of rape victims and their families across Europe. Hans-Pieter is the President of the foundation and his wife, Arlette, is the Vice-President. The foundation raised €50,000 from its fundraising concert in Galway and, at the express wish of Hans-Pieter and Arlette, that money will now be spent helping the victims of violence in the West of Ireland.

6

Sheola Keaney

'You could have been famous'

No one will ever know precisely why Thomas Kennedy (twenty-one) chose to kill his ex-girlfriend, Sheola Keaney (nineteen), as she walked back from an evening out with friends on a glorious summer evening in July 2006. But the lethal cocktail of rage, jealousy or possibly even resentment resulted in a crime that shattered the peace of a quiet Cork community – and left the Keaney family struggling to cope with the loss of their only child. For Peter and Carol Keaney, life still seems to be partly on hold from that awful July day.

Kennedy – who had initially indicated that he would contest a murder charge – subsequently pleaded guilty before the Central Criminal Court sitting. Hence, very few details of the true motivation for the crime ever emerged. The only inkling Sheola's family ever got was a statement Kennedy made to Gardaí that his strangling of the pretty student was simply done 'on the spur of the moment'.

The murder shocked the tightly knit Cork harbour town of Cobh – particularly because the killing was so senseless and perpetrated by one young person against another youngster whom he had grown up alongside. Thomas Kennedy and Sheola Keaney had seemed a typical teenage couple – but friends knew that Sheola was growing apart from her ex-boyfriend and was already making plans for a future outside Cobh.

Sheola had dated Kennedy for about eighteen months before the relationship ended in May 2006. But, to all their friends at least, the split seemed to be amicable and both youngsters appeared to remain friends and cordial towards each other. Up until Sheola's death, a photograph of the two teens happily embracing for the camera lens was included on one of the pages of their Internet social networking sites.

That July, Sheola had only recently moved back to the Cork town after living for a time in Clonmel in County Tipperary. Sheola had the offer of a job in Cobh and the truth was that she missed her extended family and friends. The Keaney family was extremely well known in Cobh – Sheola's uncle, Vincent, hit national headlines when he won the National Lottery's Lotto jackpot draw in 1994 and then used some of the proceeds of his €1.3 million win to help build the *Titanic* restaurant in the old White Star Line offices in the harbour town. Vincent's bold dream generated international headlines and he even went so far as to purchase authentic *Titanic* memorabilia for his new restaurant. (Sadly, the restaurant – like its cruise-liner namesake – foundered and eventually closed.)

Sheola loved being back in the Cork harbour town. She quickly settled back into life in Cobh from south Tipperary and regaled her friends with stories of her ambitious plans for third level studies – and her love of fashion and clothing. Many of Sheola's friends had been acquaintances since childhood – and she had not realised how much she had missed them all. It was a magical summer for the teen because she knew her next move would be to Cork city or maybe Dublin, depending on where she got her college place.

The previous day –13 July 2006 – had brought glorious sunshine sweeping across Ireland. Youngsters everywhere were enjoying parties, barbeques and beach bonfires as Ireland revelled in the heatwave. On a sunny day, Cobh – with its dramatic views over Cork Harbour – could be a stunning place to socialise and every young person in the town was planning to make the most of the Mediterranean-like sunshine. Sheola, on her return, had got a job working as a waitress in the Rushbrooke Hotel. It was a nice place to work – the staff enjoyed a good rapport with each other and the wages were reasonably good. It gave Sheola a welcome chance to save up for her third level studies.

Sheola was a popular member of staff and noted for her hard work and time keeping. Management noted that she always seemed to be smiling and never complained about any tasks she was asked to do. It was an outlook that won her the admiration of both workmates and hotel guests alike. Sheola's plan now was to save enough money to help fund college studies in the forthcoming year. In the interim, she was living in a house in Glenanaar in Cobh with her mother, Carol. It was an arrangement that worked very well because there were times when Sheola and Carol seemed more like sisters than mother and daughter.

Sheola – with her evening free – decided to go out socialising with friends on 13 July. She had several options ranging from discos to pub beach parties but the one she chose was a house party organised by some close friends in Cobh. There would be good music, plenty of chat and a chance to catch up on all the news she'd been missing out on over the days she had been working. But, because she was rostered to work in the Rushbrooke Hotel the next day, Sheola decided to head home early, leaving her friends at the house party. Somewhere on her way back to Glenanaar in the early hours of 14 July, she met up with her ex-boyfriend, Thomas Kennedy. It was to prove a fateful meeting. The last independent sighting of Sheola was of her walking with Thomas Kennedy. But the teen never made it home to Glenanaar alive.

Sheola's failure to return home and her non-appearance for work the next day immediately set alarm bells ringing. The nineteen-year-old was extremely dependable and never stayed out without telling her mother precisely where she was. The non-show was completely out of character and her family were immediately concerned. Carol instantly knew there was something seriously wrong and began ringing family and friends to see if anybody had seen Sheola or knew where she was. When a quick search failed to locate her, the Gardaí were notified and a huge search operation was launched, assisted by locals and friends of the teen. Gardaí quickly enlisted the assistance of the Irish Coastguard, Civil Defence, Cork Coastal Rescue and even the Defence Forces (there is a major Naval Service base on Haulbowline Island directly across from Cobh).

Within twenty-four hours, news of the missing teen had reached the media. Local and national newspapers reported on the disappearance and Cork radio stations carried details of the search effort and Garda appeals for information as to Sheola's whereabouts or anyone who might have seen her.

Two days later, on 16 July, the worst fears of everyone in the town were realised when Sheola's body was discovered. Her remains were found on O'Brien's Lane at Norwood Hill, Newtown, directly behind Cobh Pirate's rugby pitch and just a couple of hundred metres from her home. It was also just a couple of hundred metres from the home of her former boyfriend, Thomas Kennedy. The grim discovery was made at 8.30 p.m. – after the search had been deliberately targeted on the area where Gardaí found Sheola's distinctive shoes and handbag in the vicinity shortly after 4 p.m. that day.

The young woman's body was discovered wrapped in plastic that had been weighted down by metal railing bars and then covered with hedge clippings. The laneway ran behind a terrace of local houses and it was commonplace for residents to dump their hedge and grass cuttings over their rear walls into the laneway. The placement of the hedge clippings may have been accidental but the metal bars had clearly been deliberately placed across the plastic so as to hold it in place and conceal the teen's body. The combination of heat and moisture had accelerated the decomposition process, but

Gardaí were still able to ascertain quickly that Sheola had met a violent death. It was also apparent, given the condition of the body on its discovery, that Sheola had most likely been killed shortly after she had left her friends.

Gardaí learned from a post mortem examination conducted by Assistant State Pathologist, Dr Margaret Bolster, that the cause of the teen's death had been strangulation. A murder hunt was immediately launched by Cobh Gardaí. Sheola's Requiem Mass in St Colman's Cathedral a few days later brought the entire town to a standstill – and the then Bishop of Cloyne, Dr John Magee, directly appealed to the killer to surrender themselves to the Gardaí and to start repaying the debt to society for the evil act they had committed. A notable absentee from St Colman's Cathedral that day was Sheola's former boyfriend, Thomas Kennedy.

Dr Magee's appeal carried particular significance because, in January 2005, the bishop had made a similar appeal after the death of Midleton schoolboy, Robert Holohan (eleven), and the discovery of his remains after a massive search in a ditch near Inch, County Cork. Within twenty-four hours of Dr Magee's appeal, Gardaí made an arrest. In Cobh, locals wondered whether history was now going to repeat itself with an arrest within days of Sheola's burial. Dr Magee was eloquent in his appeal to the killer to immediately surrender to the Gardaí.

'Life is a gift from God to be cherished and respected, to be lived to the full and enjoyed, never to be rejected or taken away. When the life of a person, especially of one so young and vibrant as Sheola, is taken away in so horrific and painful circumstances, the whole of human society is shocked into silence – the silence of indignation and horror. May the one who has been responsible for this heinous crime of taking from Sheola what was most precious to her, her life, come forward and face up to the consequences involved. To pay the debt to society that has been incurred and to seek the mercy and forgiveness of the all-loving and merciful God,' Dr Magee said.

Thomas Kennedy of 84 Russell Heights, Cobh, County Cork was arrested by detectives on Friday 21 July – just twenty-four hours after Sheola's burial and one week after she had been killed. Later that evening, the young man was brought before a special sitting of Midleton District Court and charged with the murder of the pretty waitress.

Moments before Judge Michael Pattwell entered the courtroom, a young woman – a close friend of Sheola's – had to be dragged outside after she charged at Kennedy in the dock, screaming obscenities. Clearly distraught, the young woman had to be restrained by three men. She was taken outside the court, sobs echoing in her wake. Calm was restored only when Sheola's father stood up and publicly pleaded for quiet: 'For Sheola's sake, please show dignity,' Peter pleaded. But Gardaí and detectives still kept a precautionary cordon in front of the accused throughout the brief proceedings. Kennedy, who kept his head bowed throughout the entire hearing, simply told Gardaí when he was arrested, cautioned and charged with the offence: 'Plead guilty, like, I suppose.'

Kennedy was remanded in custody with his murder trial set for the following December. On 31 July, he had to receive emergency medical treatment after being savagely attacked in Cork Prison by other inmates. The young man was hospitalised with facial injuries and received five stitches to a face wound. Kennedy was later transferred to another jail for his own safety.

The first inkling of what had happened to Sheola came on 27 November when Cork Coroner's Court adjourned an inquest into the teen's death in light of the forthcoming murder trial. However, the adjournment only took place after the cause of death was given: it emerged that Sheola died from manual strangulation. Dr Bolster confirmed to the inquest that the young woman died from 'asphyxiation due to manual strangulation in association with traumatic asphyxia'.

Thomas Kennedy's trial for murder opened before the Central Criminal Court, sitting in Cork, on Tuesday 28 November 2006. It was the second high-profile murder trial to be held at the Washington Street courthouse in the space of twelve months since it was re-opened following a €25 million revamp in 2005.

Kennedy pleaded not guilty to murder. The prosecution then said that the trial could last up to three weeks with a total of 150 witnesses listed to offer evidence. The State opened the case the following Friday (1 December) with Patrick McCarthy SC, for the State (now a High Court judge), revealing for the first time that the semen of the accused, Thomas Kennedy, was found on the strangled body of his former girlfriend. Semen traces were found on both her body and on her underwear.

When her body was found under the plastic sheeting held down by steel railings, the teen was fully clothed although her trousers were partially pulled down and her top was pulled up slightly over her abdomen. It also emerged that one of

Sheola's friends had left her in Thomas Kennedy's company in the early hours of 14 July – and the nineteen-year-old was not seen alive again.

The prosecution said that its case would be based on forensic and technical evidence – and on 'half truths' and 'lies' told by the defendant, which, Mr McCarthy said, would be singled out as 'evidence of guilt'. Kennedy had told Gardaí that Sheola's death was an accident – and that he panicked after realising she was dead and decided to conceal the body. However, the prosecution said that while Sheola may have been placed in an arm-lock at one point – as Kennedy claimed – the pathology evidence indicated that the 'core point' in her death was manual strangulation.

Kennedy, who appeared in court wearing a dark suit, a white shirt and blue tie, kept his head bowed throughout the State's opening and did not look over to the public gallery where members of the Keaney family, led by Sheola's father, Peter, were gathered to hear the evidence.

The trial entered its second day on Tuesday 5 December – and Thomas Kennedy dramatically asked to be re-arraigned. He then stunned the crowded courtroom by changing his plea to guilty on the murder charge – which meant a mandatory life sentence. Kennedy offered no explanation or motivation for the brutal killing of his former girlfriend. When questioned by Gardaí as part of their original investigation, he merely said that the fatal strangling was done 'on the spur of the moment'. Now, there would be no cross-examination of Kennedy's motive or claim as to what precisely had happened.

In his initial Garda interviews, Kennedy had offered two different stories to detectives as to what had happened.

Initially, he said that Sheola had accompanied him back to his house in the early hours of 14 July and had then slept in his sister's room before leaving, on her own, at 10 a.m. the next morning. He insisted to Gardaí that the couple had spent most of the night chatting. Later, his story varied when he told Gardaí that Sheola had stayed overnight in his house but that they then had consensual sex the following morning before breakfast. He had then gone for a walk with her but had suddenly and without warning grabbed her from behind, pulling his arm tight across her throat and neck. Kennedy claimed he had then panicked when he realised after Sheola collapsed motionless at his feet that she was dead. He had then hidden her body in a state of panic and shock.

But the court heard that marks found on Sheola's neck indicated that the pretty student had, in fact, fought desperately for her life. There were indications that, as well as the pressure on her neck, she may have suffered mechanical asphyxia, which is the process whereby someone cannot breathe because their chest movement is restricted such as by having someone kneel or sit on top of them. This could have taken place in conjunction with the manual strangulation.

The sentencing hearing took place the following day, Wednesday 5 December. The 24-hour adjournment had been sought by the defence counsel to allow him an opportunity to take instructions from his client. Kennedy would receive a mandatory life sentence but, before the term was formally imposed, the court heard victim impact statements from her parents, Carol and Peter. Carol's statement provoked sobs from the packed courtroom where Sheola's friends and workmates struggled to contain their emotions at the heart-rending revelations being made. Carol, too, struggled to compose herself as she explained to the court precisely what Thomas Kennedy's actions had done to her family.

'It was four days before you were taken from the spot where he left you. Did he realise the effect that sight would have on me – to see the state you were in after being left there for so long? Your poor body had been exposed to the [July] heat for four days and it had decomposed so much that your friends and family were not allowed to see you to say goodbye.'

'I lived for you from the moment you were born – and it is unbearable to remember all those things about you growing up. I sometimes dream that I get to the place where you died just in time to save you – only to wake up and to realise that you are gone. I dread to think how you suffered – I try to block it out, you poor child.

'You used to say that everybody loved you – the first day I went up to water the flowers on your grave I said to myself that this is pathetic. All I can do for you now is to look after your grave and this is not right. Your cousin Alex said to me recently that Sheola could have been famous – you had such a way with people, everybody knew you. It is such a sad waste of life. Sheola, we all miss you so terribly. I love you with all my heart.'

The court had barely had time to draw its breath when a second, equally harrowing victim impact statement statement was delivered by Sheola's father, Peter. His statement left the entire courtroom silent as listeners struggled to comprehend the appalling scale of the tragedy that had been visited upon Sheola's parents. Thomas Kennedy sat silent in the dock with his head bowed, not making eye contact with anyone.

'Where do I begin to tell you about the impact that

Sheola's death has had on me? It started with a phone call to say that she was missing and from there my life, as I knew it, changed forever. I cannot fit nineteen years into a few minutes but I am going to try and explain to you what Sheola meant to me,' Peter Keaney explained to the court.

'Sheola was born on 22 January 1987 – I was at her birth and when I cradled her in my arms I thought that she was the most precious gift I had ever received. I remember when she was six years old and had a bad flu, the only thing that could make her better was her teddies, LaLa and Piggy. I was distraught at the time with worry, thinking: "What would I do if anything happened to her?" I had the same feeling of worry seventeen weeks ago but this time there was nothing that could make it better.

'Her dream was to go to college to do business studies – to earn loads of money and travel the world. She had a very outgoing personality and excelled at many things, majorettes, swimming and hockey to name just a few. She made friends very easily and it seemed when she was young I spent my time driving her to one birthday party or another. I remember her first day at school: she was bursting to go in and get started. When she came home she refused to take off her uniform.

'Sheola never lost that enthusiasm for living and doing new things and she carried it through to the end of her short life. When my child was born nineteen years ago my role as a father was to mind her, to protect her, to guide her and to love her. I did not always get it right. But she was my reason for getting up in the morning. On the day she made her First Holy Communion I remember looking at her in the church and thinking to myself that the next time I see her in a white dress it will be her wedding day and how proud I would be to walk her up the aisle to marry someone who would love and respect her for the person that she is.

'Now, there will be no wedding day, no twenty-first birthday, no graduation and no grandchildren. I will not be getting any postcards from Australia, Thailand or America to say, "Hey Dad, look where I am!" All this was taken from me on 14 July. There is a huge void in my life now that my child is dead – I wake up every morning and think I am after having a nightmare and then reality sets in with a bang. The realisation [is] that I will never be able to see or talk to her again in this lifetime. I find it impossible to live with. Since the brutal way Sheola was taken from me I am now left a broken man – I am unable to focus on work as I cannot make sense of what has happened. Without the help of medication, counselling and the support of my family and friends I would not be able to carry on.

'People tell me that time is a great healer but I struggle with this as every waking hour I have is spent thinking about Sheola and what happened to her and what should have been. I think about how much I love her and how much I miss her. I cannot describe to you in words the heartache and pain that I am in since my daughter's death. To lose a child through illness or accident in heartbreaking but to lose a child in the way I did, with her basic right to life so cruelly and so unjustly taken away from her, has left me devastated. I just want you [all] to know that I love my daughter.'

As the trial ended and Kennedy was led away to begin his life sentence, the true enormity of what Carol and Peter Keaney faced suddenly struck home. They had lost Sheola, their only child, and nothing could ever erase that fact. In the days after the murder trial, as the dust slowly settled, that was the stark, tragic reality they were left to face. They adopted different policies in their coping mechanisms. Carol has largely remained silent, never publicly commenting beyond what she revealed in her victim impact statement. In contrast, Peter got publicly involved with the victim support group, AdVIC (Advocates for Victims of Homicide), and repeatedly spoke out on issues impacting on victims' families and criminal reform.

His experience of the judicial system and its failings made him determined to campaign for a better system. 'I just didn't want anyone to go through what we went through. You don't realise what it is like until you are caught in the middle of it. The Gardaí are usually great but the reality is that you have to fight for even the smallest bits of information. It seems as if the entire system is there to protect the rights of the perpetrator – and does its best to ignore you when the trial is over.'

He made appearances on TV3 and RTÉ, including *The Late Late Show*. He commented to both Newstalk and 96FM on various proposed changes in the judicial system over the treatment of victims and their right to be heard before the courts. One of the first major comments he made was about victim impact statements, which, it was now proposed, would be revised and better grounded in law so as to protect the right of victims' families to be heard.

'I think it is a very positive move forward – I think these changes badly need to be made,' Peter explained. 'I think that victim impact statements are effectively the last voice you can offer your loved one. So the judge, the jury and the general public can hear you give a voice to your loved one. These statements also allow families to get across exactly the impact that the loss of your child or loved one has had on your entire family.'

Peter also actively campaigned for people to get involved in AdVIC and for families who have suffered the loss of a loved one through violent crime to be able to offer support, sympathy and understanding to other families. Peter has also become a regular attendee at special memorial events for the victims of violent crime in Ireland.

'I don't want anyone to go through what we have gone through,' he said. 'That's why we are highlighting this issue so that proper help can be provided for people when they need it most.' Peter has also become an outspoken advocate of the need for special support and counselling contact lines – amid the hope that these can serve as a place of last resort for those who may be contemplating a violent crime or who may find themselves under emotional or psychological pressure and fear the potential consequences.

Such efforts helped give Peter a focus although they could not completely dull the pain of realising what he had lost. Peter marked Sheola's twenty-first birthday by placing flowers on her grave in Cobh and then attending a special memorial Mass in 2008. He was touched by the fact that so many of Sheola's friends – all of whom were now busy with their own lives and studies – still took time to remember the friend they had lost two years earlier. Peter admitted that there are days when the pain and suffering wash over him like giant waves.

'It is something that hits you every hour of the day – people talk about healing and forgiveness but those words don't mean a lot when you know your child was stolen from you. People tell you that time is a healer. But you never really get over something like this. How can you ever forget that your only child was murdered? How can you ever forget that?' he asked. 'People mean well – I know they do. But they just don't understand the suffering and the sense of loss. There are no words to ease what the families of the victims of violent crime go through. I will never again get to chat with Sheola – to see her smile or to live out her life. I won't get to see her live the life that I had dreamed she would have. That kind of pain just never goes away. It is always there.

'I have a photograph of her by my bedside table. Her face is the last thing that I see at night and the first thing that I see in the morning. But it means an awful lot to know how much Sheola was loved and how much she is missed. That is one thing that definitely helps – to know just how many people cared about Sheola in her brief life and how many people still miss her.'

For Peter the process of adjusting to life without his beloved daughter has been fraught and painful. In January 2008, he reacted with fury to the confirmation that a Johnny Cash tribute show was being arranged for inmates of Mountjoy Prison. In an interview with Newstalk's Southern Correspondent, Jonathan Healy, he expressed total bewilderment with the fixation some people have about making life easier for inmates.

'It is an absolute disgrace – these people are in there to do time because they did a crime. Why should they get all the benefits? I'm totally irate over it. If I want to go to a concert I have to pay €50 or €60 for a ticket and travel to it and then pay accommodation. But they [Mountjoy Prison] bring them in for them and give them a good time.

'If you take someone's life, how can you be regarded as a human being? They should be sent up to Connemara or Donegal and made to fill in potholes so as to give something back to [the] society from which they took.'

When interviewed for this book, Peter stressed that the lack of information and support for the families of violent crime victims in Ireland is something that urgently needs to be highlighted. 'You want to know what we are told? Absolutely nothing. That's what happened after the trial. If I want to know when the man who strangled and killed my daughter is going to be released I have to write to a liaison officer. That information will not be volunteered to me.

'I was told to get counselling after the trial was over but no one was able to tell me where to go or who to ask for. There are some good services in Dublin but there is not a lot else nationwide. That has to change. There is little or no support for families and that is simply not good enough.

'No one ever came knocking on my door after the trial to ask if I was OK. No one ever checked to see if I had found a suitable counsellor or if I still had any questions. Since the day the trial finished, no one from the judicial system has come near me. I've been offered no support services. But the man who killed my Sheola gets three square meals every single day, he has a right to an education in custody and he has access to a psychiatrist or doctor if he ever needs it. That is how the system deals with the families of victims. It seems to me that the perpetrators have all the rights.'

Today, Peter is determined to fight for a better system

for families and those scarred by violent crime. Most of all, he wants to see a proper nationwide system of counsellors experienced in dealing with the aftermath of violent crime and specially trained in helping the families left behind. 'The problem is that even if you find a counsellor to help, the chances are that while they might have dealt with grieving issues to do with a family death, they have never, ever encountered the raw pain of those who lost a loved one to violent crime. They ask: "How did your daughter die?" Then you tell them your daughter was strangled and murdered – and you can see them go pale in front of you.'

Peter is convinced that, if people knew exactly how the system works in Ireland, they would be appalled – and immediately demand change on behalf of victim's families. 'There is no need for it – all people want is the right to information, the right to supports and the right to be informed of what is going on. No one wants to interfere with the trial process or the delivery of justice. But why do families have to go chasing information when the trial is over?' he asked.

He also added that issues about how victims' families dress during trial proceedings – often a factor in trial coverage for the broadcast media – should be no concern whatsoever for the judiciary. 'If families dress well it is because they see it as a mark of respect for the loved one they lost. People dress well at communions, confirmations and weddings to show respect – why shouldn't they dress well if they are attending a court hearing relating to their loved one? If they link arms going into a court or coming out of a court, it is nothing more than them showing each other solidarity and support. Nothing more.'

7

Roy Collins

'The world is a dangerous place not because of those
who do evil but because of those who look on and do
nothing.'

Roy Collins (thirty-five) simply never stood a chance. His
killer was just too close to evade – and he had nowhere to run
in the tight confines of the Limerick arcade he managed. He
had nothing to hand with which to defend himself – and the
attack was so unexpected his killer had come within feet of
him before Roy even realised what was going on. The young
father-of-two was confronted by gunman James Dillon
(twenty-four) shortly before noon in the popular amusement
arcade which he operated in the Roxboro Shopping Centre

on Holy Thursday 9 April 2009. It was an encounter Roy Collins would not survive.

Dillon – who was of no fixed abode but originally from the southside of Limerick city – was a relatively recent recruit to the McCarthy–Dundon gang, one of Limerick's most feared and ruthless crime organisations. His task was not to rob Roy Collins but to kill him. It was a simple, ruthless and cold-blooded act of retaliation and revenge – designed by the gang bosses to warn the entire city that anyone who stood up to them faced dire consequences. It was effectively a declaration of war on civilised Limerick and Irish society.

Roy's father, Steve, was a native of Dublin who had built up several successful businesses in Limerick. The father of four was a popular figure around the city – he was respected both for his business acumen and his support for Limerick's campaign of urban and social regeneration, which got into gear in the early 1980s. Because of his involvement in the pub and arcade businesses, Steve had developed a knack for dealing with people and there were few in Limerick who did not know or like the Dubliner. But the Collins family's quiet existence was shattered in December 2004 when Steve's adopted son, Ryan Lee, refused to allow Annabel Dundon, who was then just fourteen years old, into the family's pub, Brannigan's. Ryan was reasonable but firm – she was just too young to be allowed onto the licensed premises, given the new regulations, which were being firmly enforced by the Gardaí.

However, Annabel's brother, Wayne (twenty-four), was not a man used to dealing with refusals. He wasn't willing to listen to explanations and demanded that his sister be allowed in. When she was again refused, Wayne Dundon was furious and immediately threatened to kill Lee. Dundon left the scene, staring icily at the young pub worker. Just over thirty minutes later, a gunman wearing a motorcycle helmet walked into Brannigan's and singled Lee out behind the bar counter.

The nineteen-year-old pub worker was shot once and then, after the gunman initially walked away only to callously return, was shot a second time. Because of the difficulty in identifying the gunman, no one was ever charged with the shooting. But Wayne Dundon was jailed for ten years for having threatened Lee outside the pub. The Court of Criminal Appeal later reduced the sentence to seven years and Wayne Dundon was released from Wheatfield Prison in March 2010. The sentence was imposed after the barman testified in court – despite vicious anonymous threats delivered to the Collins family about the dire consequences of what would happen if he did.

The Collins family had been unwittingly pitched into the middle of a gangland war that was threatening to tear Limerick apart. The combination of social deprivation, insane housing policies and the plague of drug addiction ultimately created fertile ground for the evolution of powerful gangs on Shannonside. Limerick's gangs soon earned a ferocious reputation for violence – all spawned by the huge profits being generated by the drugs trade.

When the city's dominant drug gang split into rival factions, a third gang moved into the vacuum and a spate of assassinations marked the beginning of a bloody turf war. The Keane–Collopy and McCarthy–Dundon–Ryan feud had, by 2010, directly or indirectly claimed almost twenty lives and sparked a national debate about how to counter organised crime. Irish society reeled with stunning revelations about crime empires being run from prison cells and attempts to smuggle military-grade weaponry into Ireland in a bid to wipe out rivals. Limerick's gangs were now trying to arm themselves to a degree comparable to most European armies.

When the stolen black Mercedes carrying James Dillon pulled up outside the Roxboro Shopping Centre at lunchtime on 9 April 2009, the brutal act about to be committed was all about events that had happened five years earlier. Dillon was driven to the scene by one of the McCarthy–Dundon gang's most vicious younger gunmen. He was there in part to help Dillon but also to ensure that the young man carried out the shooting he had been ordered to undertake. The man was also closely associated with the murder of Shane Geoghegan, a young rugby player who was killed after being shot in a case of mistaken identity the previous November. The grim reality was that, had James Dillon got cold feet about the murder he had been ordered to commit, it is most likely he would himself have been shot.

Dillon got out of the Mercedes and walked quickly into the Coin Castle amusement arcade. He never even realised that Roy's father, Steve, was working in an office in the Steering Wheel pub, adjacent to the Roxboro arcade. Since the events of 2004/2005, Steve had been receiving round-the-clock Garda protection. In fact, he had been escorted to the Steering Wheel pub shortly after 9.30 a.m. to begin work that morning by two armed detectives, so seriously were the threats levelled against him taken by Gardaí.

If Dillon had second thoughts about the brutal task assigned to him, he overcame his doubts. Having confronted an unsuspecting Roy Collins – and, despite the fact the arcade and shopping centre were quickly filling up with patrons – Dillon fired a single shot from a revolver at close range. The high velocity bullet struck Roy Collins in the upper torso and tore out through the young man's back, leaving a gaping exit wound. Dillon immediately fled back to the waiting Mercedes. The car hurtled off at speed – in fact, so recklessly was the vehicle subsequently driven across Limerick city that it crashed no fewer than four times before it was finally abandoned.

The Garda response to news of the shooting was swift and professional. Armed officers raced to the Ballinacurra–Weston area that was the stronghold of the McCarthy–Dundon gang, with immediate suspicions about who might be responsible for the brutal attack. One Garda unit spotted the two suspects who immediately separated and fled on foot. An armed Garda response team, equipped with a warrant, later found James Dillon crouched under a bunk bed in an upstairs bedroom of a terraced house.

Dillon had not had time to change clothes and burn the garments he had been wearing at the Roxboro Shopping Centre. It was a crucial mistake and a major breakthrough for detectives. Garda technical experts later confirmed the presence of firearm residue on Dillon's dark-coloured hoodie and a glove found near where he was hiding. Gardaí also knew that the house in which he was arrested was closely associated with the McCarthy–Dundon gang.

Back in the Coin Castle arcade, Roy Collins was desperately fighting for life in a rapidly-spreading pool of his own blood. His father, Steve, was horrified when a panicked woman ran into his office in the Steering Wheel pub and shouted that someone was hurt and bleeding on the floor of the amusement arcade. Steve raced to the scene, an icy ball of fear growing in his stomach. Initially, he thought there might have been a fight but his worst nightmare became a reality when he recognised his eldest son lying prone on the floor.

'I ran into the casino and Roy was lying on the floor. He was shot in the back and was crouched over and couldn't get his breath. He was trying to talk to me but I told him to stop talking. I picked him up, he said: "Dad, I can't breathe." I said "take it easy, son". I turned him on his side as he was uncomfortable. I just waited with him for the ambulance and the police. He told me he was after being shot,' Steve said.

'I had seen that the bullet on the ground had just gone through him. He was frightened, frightened of dying. I didn't know what to do. I held him and waited and waited. All he said to me was: "I love you, Da – and tell Mum I love her." He was just worried that he was going to die. I told him he wasn't. I didn't think he was at that point,' Steve added. The horrified father did his best to comfort his wounded son as they waited for the ambulance to arrive.

By the time paramedics reached the scene, Steve was cradling his son in his arms while surrounded by a spreading pool of blood. Roy was now slipping into unconsciousness due to acute blood loss. Paramedics frantically worked on Roy as he was raced to the nearby Limerick Regional Hospital in preparation for emergency surgery. But the damage was simply too great. Despite the best efforts of surgeons, the young man died shortly after being admitted.

Few killings triggered such an outpouring of grief and

outrage as the murder of Roy Collins. The fact that the killing had been a deliberate, calculated and cold-blooded act of revenge aimed at warning law-abiding citizens of the consequences of challenging the evil gang bosses made the murder almost unique in modern Irish criminal history. It was as premeditated as it was pointless. The entire nation was outraged.

Public anger over the murder prompted a massive city centre demonstration which was ultimately attended by more than 5,000 people. The Chairman of Limerick's Joint Policing Committee, Kevin Kiely, helped organise the demonstration in conjunction with the City Council and the Collins family. Steve Collins welcomed the support for his family and was unstinting in his praise for the Gardaí but said a consistent campaign of support for the Gardaí was needed rather than emotional one-off events. 'I think the march was effective. Everybody is talking about the McCarthy–Dundons and the terror they are bringing to this city here. They have ruined this city and everybody is so angry about it. There are so many nice and good people down here and they are being sullied with this stick and they are sick of it now,' he said.

Kevin Kiely said it was vital that ordinary people give their voice to demands for the gang activity to stop and show their revulsion at the bloodshed. 'We want the people of Limerick to show solidarity to the Collins family and families who have been victims to these criminal gangs in Limerick over the years. We want as much support as possible from across Limerick and all organisations to send a message back to these people that they are not wanted on the streets of Limerick,' Mr Kiely said.

Yet, despite the marches and the public outrage, the gang

bosses were not deterred. In a chilling riposte, Steve Collins Jnr (twenty-seven) received a death threat just over a fortnight after his brother's murder. Gardaí stepped up their protection of the entire Collins family while the government rushed in new anti-organised-crime legislation. For the first time, organised crime could be dealt with by the Special Criminal Court, which had previously only dealt with paramilitary offences. The Gardaí were promised whatever resources they needed for cracking down on the feuding Limerick gangs and elite Garda teams including the Emergency Response Unit (ERU) began extended operations on Shannonside. Justice Minister Dermot Ahern personally contacted Steve Collins and later described the murder of Roy Collins as 'a watershed moment' in Ireland's battle against crime.

Steve Collins was adamant that no one was going to drive him and his family out of Limerick. 'Anything we require from the Gardaí, they give us. They review all our security and have been very good. We feel a lot safer,' he said. 'It was only after the march that we have time to reflect on our lives and what we would do. When you reflect on it and think about it, the time if we were ever going to move off [from Limerick] was after what happened to Ryan and we didn't do it then.

'All the unfortunate things that have happened to us afterwards – it wouldn't be the time and it wouldn't be right for us just to run away from these now, not in my son's memory, I would never do that, no. I am not going to move from here. We have to stay now and fight for justice and make things safer for ourselves but they are not going to run us away, no way,' Steve vowed.

In May 2010, James Dillon appeared before the Central Criminal Court and, despite initial indications of a protracted trial, the young man entered a guilty plea to Roy Collin's murder. It transpired that Dillon had been interviewed by Gardaí a total of twenty-six separate times at Henry Street Garda Station following his arrest. He had initially refused to comment but the crucial moment came when his grandfather visited him in custody. The man had helped raise James Dillon and was one of the people he was closest to. After their conversation, Dillon simply told Gardaí: 'I shot Roy Collins.'

Yet James Dillon was little more than a pawn for the Limerick crime gangs. The young man had first run foul of the law at nineteen years of age. After a spate of relatively minor convictions for Road Traffic Act (RTA) breaches and public order offences, he suddenly moved into the orbit of the McCarthy–Dundon gang. The shooting of Roy Collins was, in essence, a task to 'prove' himself to the gang bosses. The gang leaders had evolved the classic technique of distancing themselves from major acts of violence – that was left to minor and often expendable minions.

Dillon was terrified of the gang chiefs and so feared their anger that he steadfastly refused to cooperate with Gardaí about the identity of who had driven the stolen Mercedes getaway car after the Roxboro shooting that day. Limerick had already seen the murder of the driver of one getaway car from a gangland shooting because the young man was viewed to represent too great a risk if interrogated by Gardaí.

For James Dillon, a life sentence now beckoned. The young man had been tempted by the supposedly glamorous world of Limerick's drug gangs – plenty of drugs, access to ready cash, the use of powerful cars, 'respect' on the streets (which was, in fact, nothing more than abject fear), not to mention the promise of women and foreign holidays. It was a world totally removed from the decent upbringing his grandparents had offered him. James Dillon had been brought up in Kennedy Park on Limerick's south side and was immersed in sports. He developed into a very talented underage hurler with Old Christians GAA Club and also played with Sexton Street CBS. He would even go on to play schoolboy soccer in Limerick and show enough promise to be asked to consider try-outs for senior sides.

His grandparents were also determined that James would get a decent education for himself. He sat both his Junior Cert and his Leaving Cert. He then enrolled in a FÁS course and began training as an apprentice butcher. But when he was eighteen, the lure of Limerick's underworld became too strong to resist. Personal use of drugs and alcohol accelerated the transition and, by the time he was twenty-three, James Dillon had acquired thirteen criminal convictions, most for public order and traffic offences. In September 2008, he appeared before Limerick District Court on a drugs charge. Within four weeks, he had moved out of his grandparent's house and disappeared into the labyrinthine world of Ballinacurra–Weston, which was controlled by the McCarthy–Dundons. James Dillon was now staying in gang accommodation – and, while he may not have realised it, he was being groomed for bigger, more violent things.

Facing into a life sentence, James Dillon also knew that his former gang associates would not hesitate for a second to turn on his friends and family if he broke the Omertà code of silence they enforced at gunpoint. He would do his life sentence, behave himself in prison and hope that the Parole Board took a lenient view of his application for release in a decade or so. But he would not say a word to Gardaí about who was in the Mercedes with him on Holy Thursday – even if it meant the prospect of having time slashed from his prison term.

For Steve Collins, there was scant consolation in seeing Dillon receive a life sentence. '[He was just] an idiot who was carrying out an order. These people [the gang bosses] are cowards, as far as I am concerned. They won't go and do these things themselves. They get the likes of James Dillon to go and do it – an idiot. I know there was a group of other people involved in this murder and I would like to think if the evidence was gathered and if somebody else came forward with more information that they would be brought to justice because we are dealing with terrible people here – they are a menace to society,' he said.

The father of four's victim impact statement to the Central Criminal Court painted a heart-rending picture of the price a decent, honourable family had paid for standing up to the gangland thugs and trying to do the right thing for both Limerick and Irish society.

'How can I put into words the impact that the loss of our beloved son Roy has had on the family?' Steve told the Central Criminal Court. 'A devastating, numb feeling that I know will be with us until the day we meet our maker. Roy was a hard-working man – a productive member of society just putting the finishing touches to his dream home, a house he built for himself on the lake in Killaloe-Ballina – security for

Monica Butler in 2005: the pain over the loss of her only child is still clearly etched on her face. (Provision)

John Butler (left) with his father, John Snr, on the night of his school ball. Four years later, John would be shot in cold blood. In 2006, his father would take his own life, unable to deal with the aftermath of his son's killing. (Courtesy Monica Butler)

Celine Cawley had forged successful careers as a model, an actress and had built up her own successful film production company. A devoted mother, she died at the hands of her husband, Eamon Lillis. (*Irish Independent*)

The family of slain mother-of-one Meg Walsh struggle to come to terms with the horror of her killing. Meg's daughter, Sasha (centre), and her brother, James (left), are pictured escorting Meg's coffin outside Killavullen parish church in north Cork. (Provision)

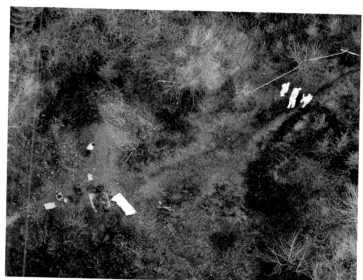

An aerial view of the isolated woodland at Kilbrittain in west Cork where widow Ann Corcoran's body was found by Gardaí. The remains had been burned and then covered with stones, twigs and branches in a shallow grave. Note Garda forensic experts in white to the right of the picture. (Provision)

Oliver Hayes, head covered by a hood, is led into a special sitting of Bandon District Court by detectives on 6 February 2009. (Provision)

Manuela Riedo (seventeen), as beautiful in personality as she was in looks. Her trip to Galway was supposed to be the first of many overseas trips for a Swiss teen determined to see the world. It was her tragic misfortune to meet arguably the most dangerous man in Galway while on her own just three days into her Irish trip. (*Irish Independent*)

Loyal, generous, fun-loving and totally devoted to her family, Sheola Keaney went out to enjoy the glorious sunshine of 13 July 2006 in her native Cobh, County Cork, but met her death at the hands of her ex-boyfriend as she walked home. (Provision)

Sheola Keaney's funeral: her parents are obscured behind the flower-bedecked hearse. Just 24 hours after Sheola was buried, her ex-boyfriend, Thomas Kennedy, was arrested and subsequently charged with her murder. (Provision)

Roy Collins was brutally shot and killed simply because his family had taken a stand for justice and the rule of law in crime-torn Limerick. (Press 22)

Steve Collins, photographed here in his family's pub, still cannot comprehend the utter senselessness of his son's killing. (Press 22)

The du Plantier family photographed in happier times: Sophie poses at a French film ball with her husband, Daniel (right), and son, Pierre-Louis (left). (Provision)

Sophie's mother, Marguerite Bouniol, prays at a candlelit memorial at Toormore in west Cork in December 2008. (Provision)

Mariusz Szwajkos (left) and Pawel Kalite (right) both died after being stabbed in the head with a screwdriver by a Dublin teen who had been drinking and taking drugs. Mariusz was killed after bravely going to his friend's aid. (*Irish Independent*)

A picture that perfectly captures the friendly, kind and jovial personality of retired bar worker Donal Manley. He was brutally battered to death in his own home in Cork in October 2008. (Provision)

his children [Shannon, thirteen, and Charlie, nine] looking forward to a bright future together.

'Now, every day we look at Roy's two beautiful daughters lost in confusion as to where their daddy has gone, their little hearts broken beyond repair, too young to understand, too afraid to contemplate what's gone on and why.' Roy's partner, Melissa Crawford, broke down and wept as Steve outlined the trauma surrounding the loss of his son.

'To Roy, they were his life – they meant everything to him. He was a wonderful father to them and they have been left to go on into life without him and I know they will miss him every day. I look at Roy's mother every day, the grief etched in her face, a heartbroken shell of her former self. We try to comfort each other to keep strong for our children. We just cannot believe this has happened to us. No parent should have to bury their children – it is not natural.

'Roy's brothers' and sisters' lives changed on that terrible day. They now live a life of fear – always looking over their shoulder, terrified of what could happen to them and all because we did the right thing. We did our civic duty and paid the ultimate price. Evil came into our lives on that fateful day and took the love of our lives in a callous act, a cowardly act, an unforgivable act, a total waste of a good life.'

Steve Collins said that the utter futility of his son's murder was the hardest thing to comprehend. 'The impact this had had on the nation is of disbelief – a sense of vulnerability and heartbreak for everyone when they look into their own children's eyes and think "there but for the Grace of God", and an understanding of what we are feeling and our loss as a family.

'I don't think Carmel, his mother, or me, his devastated dad, will ever get over this. I don't know how to get over this. I have worked all my life to give my family everything I could because at the end of the day that is what I feel life is all about – family. And if you have your health and your family, nothing else matters. There is a link gone from my life. My beautiful son, my pal, my inspiration – a boy I was so proud to call my son. Rest in Peace, Roy – [from] Dad and Mam, your girls, brothers, sisters, loved ones and friends.'

The reality is that Roy Collins' killing – just like that of Shane Geoghegan – underlined the threat to Irish society posed by organised crime gangs. Dublin gangs wield the same ruthless power over life and death as their Limerick counterparts. The lethal Drimnagh–Crumlin feud more than underlined that fact. Starkly, Garda Commissioner Fachtna Murphy acknowledged that the gangland threat had to be faced down – and would be faced down. 'But,' he said, '[there are] difficult times ahead for Limerick.'

At times, Steve Collins feels that much more could – and perhaps should – be done to isolate and tackle the gangland bosses who use minions to evade arrest. 'Internment is the only way forward now. They have talked about it and it has been shunned in the past, but now something like this has to be done. They have to be put away. You cannot win with these people . . . whether you give evidence or don't give evidence they are still going to come after you.

'We are terrified, I really thought that after killing my son they might have got their pound of flesh and they would leave us alone. But it doesn't look like they are going away. I don't know what to do any more. It is all drug related. They have made it dirty now; they are gone into intimidating people and businesses. They think they are the mafia now, they really do. They are wannabe gangsters. They think they are the kingpins, they go around talking like the mafia . . . it is just unbelievable,' he added.

Gardaí dramatically increased the protection of the Collins family after a letter claimed that a €75,000 'hit' or assassination contract had been taken out by the McCarthy–Dundon gang against Steve. The claim was made all the more chilling given that it followed reports in some Irish newspapers that the Limerick gangs were now trying to recruit foreign hit men to assassinate their Irish targets.

'It [the round-the-clock protection] is very invasive now. I am looking at guards all the time outside my house now, everywhere I go I am being followed by guards. It is not a life that anyone should have – they [the McCarthy–Dundon gang] still got to us. My son was killed at twelve o'clock in the day. You just don't know when it is going to happen,' said Steve.

His son, Steve Jnr, has found the long-term impact of the threats against him to be particularly difficult. 'It has wrecked his life. It is no life for a young man to be looking over his shoulder all the time. He can't socialise – he can do nothing. He is terrified. We are running a business, we are running a pub where every time the door opens it could be a potential assassin – it is a terrifying position to be in.' The young man now effectively avoids socialising in Limerick – and is careful about his movements, methodical in not following the same routes or establishing travel patterns that could leave him vulnerable.

The Collins family now find it most difficult to listen to well-intentioned but totally uninformed people complain about the judicial measures aimed at targeting the gang kingpins – and the Garda crackdown. 'These people need to get real – take their blinkers off and look at what is going on in the real world around them. Nobody's liberties are being trampled upon with these laws. It is about protecting people,' Steve said. 'Come down here to Limerick and live my life, which I have been left with because of these thugs. Leave the leafy estates and look at what ordinary law-abiding people have to deal with. We stood up to these gangs and look what happened.

'Ordinary people have nothing to fear. The only people who need to worry about this are the criminals, it is time to take the gangs down. Without these laws, I don't know where we will go. Anyone who talks about civil liberties being trampled upon would want to come down to Limerick and have a look at the situation in places like Weston [the strategic base for the McCarthy–Dundon gang].'

Now it seems that only time will tell if Roy Collins' murder proves to be the watershed that so many in government first claimed it to be. For the Collins family there is the ongoing pain at the loss of a beloved son and the realisation that the man jailed for the murder was little more than an automaton who simply pulled the trigger at the behest of another. The person truly responsible for Roy's death is the gang boss who ordered the killing in cold blood and who still remains free.

One year after Roy's murder, the Collins family attended a special memorial Mass and then went to Roxboro Shopping Centre for the unveiling of a special plaque in memory of their eldest son. 'It is heartbreaking, as you can imagine. It is hard to even think about it. It has been a very tough, tough year. It is our life now and we just want to get on with it. But there is not a day goes by that I don't think of Roy and wish that he was still here with us,' Steve said.

The wording of the plaque – which was erected just metres from the arcade that Roy ran – reads like a call to action to every decent citizen who does not want to see their proud city corrupted by the gang lords. It reads: 'The message is that the world is a dangerous place not because of those who do evil but because of those who look on and do nothing.'

Later that year, Steve and his family agreed to take part in a special documentary for RTÉ. The programme was part of RTÉ's *Prime Time Investigates* series and it aimed to offer viewers a graphic insight into an average day in the life of Steve and his family. The programme – broadcast on 8 July 2010 – attracted near-record audience figures and featured several moving scenes, including one where Steve attends the flower-bedecked grave of his son. For many, the programme perfectly encapsulated the nightmare facing ordinary people caught up in Limerick's escalating cycle of gang violence. For Steve, taking part in the programme was an important part of helping people understand what happened to his family – and what must not be allowed happen to other families.

Incredibly, despite all the heartache, horror and fears, Steve Collins still believes that the message will eventually get across to those who matter and that good people will stand up to be counted in the battle for Limerick's future. He is also hopeful, if a little anxious, that in the long run, the new anti-organised-crime legislation will have the same impact that the Criminal Assets Bureau (CAB) legislation did after being introduced in the wake of Veronica Guerin's gang-ordered murder in 1996. He views getting the gang bosses off the streets of Limerick and behind prison bars as the strategic key to winning the battle. Only then can urban regeneration and anti-social-disadvantage policies truly have a chance of working.

'We have to be patient. I understand that the Gardaí have to get it right. I think it is important that when it [the future prosecutions] goes across to the Special Criminal Court, that they are successful with this and get convictions. I can understand the guards and prosecution are being cautious with this but I am still anxious about it. Until people see it working, they won't have any confidence in it. So like everyone else, we are just hoping to see the new legislation working.'

But he believes that, with legal reform in train, it is now vital that Ireland turn its attention to the prison system. 'A lot of people just don't believe what has been going on. Gangsters' molls throwing drugs over the wall of a prison and prison guards being threatened and intimidated. Something needs to be done – these gangsters should view prison as a place of punishment, not a place where they can go and have a laugh with their mates.'

Steve is particularly scathing about the 25 per cent remission for good behaviour offered for convicted offenders. He argues that the remission should not be automatic but should be far more conditional – and related to assisting Gardaí with information or undergoing counselling and victim impact courses. He has also proposed that the legislation be amended so that prisoners who misbehave or threaten prison staff face the prospect of having 25 per cent added to the sentences. 'My problem is that everything seems to be stacked in their favour – there doesn't seem to be any question of people doing hard time. We need to make better use of maximum-security prisons and if people are handed sentences for violent crime or organised crime, that is where they should serve their terms.'

'There is no way the prisons should be filled with people who are being sent to jail for minor offences or not paying fines. That is ridiculous in this day and age. We need to look at the whole prison system and make sure that it is there to deal first of all with violent offenders. Prison should not be a place that criminals aren't too bothered about being sent to.'

Steve's fearless stance on victims' rights and legal reform has earned him national plaudits – but has also made him powerful enemies in the criminal world. He and his family continue to live under round-the-clock Garda protection. Having paid such a terrible price for doing the right thing, his most heartfelt wish is now his most poignant: 'We just want to be left alone – that's all. We just want to get on with our lives in peace,' he said.

8

Sophie Toscan du Plantier

'Sophie loved west Cork – it was her special place'

Toormore can be a lonely spot at any time of the year, but on a dark December evening the haunting beauty of the rugged west Cork landscape can seem almost intimidating as the brooding mountains loom overhead. The feeling is perhaps a combination of the isolation of the area, the nature of the terrain and the memories of the terrible crime committed here on a black Christmas night in 1996. It is hardly surprising then that every glimmer of light seems to represent a beacon of hope – a guide to safety.

On Monday 22 December 2008 the darkness of the evening was broken in Toormore by pinpricks of fragile light that seemed to defy the chill wind. Georges and Marguerite Bouniol were staging a candlelit vigil for their daughter, Sophie (thirty-nine), at the very spot where she had been battered to death exactly twelve years earlier.

I had arrived earlier that evening, having attended a special press conference held by Sophie's friends at Cork Airport, and filed my reports for the *Irish Independent*. But I wanted to attend the candlelit vigil in person because of the poignancy of the ceremony and the fact that, on several occasions over the years, I had met and interviewed Georges and Marguerite. When I arrived, the scene was virtually deserted save for a single parked car. *Irish Examiner* photographer Des Barry had similarly arrived early for the ceremony and we were grateful for each other's company. Des shared my views that this was a particularly lonely spot – and both of us remarked that Sophie, attacked that evening twelve years before, had simply had nowhere to escape to.

We took up position at the bottom of the steep, winding laneway that leads up to Sophie's holiday home. Just a few metres from where we stood was the simple, stone, Celtic cross that marks the spot where Sophie's battered, blood-soaked body was found. A neighbour – aware that the vigil was going to take place that night – had placed a string of battery-powered lights around the cross. By 8 p.m., members of Sophie's family and friends had come out from the house and walked down to the stone cross to prepare for the vigil. Preferring the softer light of candles, they replaced the neighbour's lights with simple candles placed inside covers to protect them from the biting wind. The effect was marked and the cross seemed to shimmer in the candlelight and shadows.

A member of the family approached us and invited us up to the house for a drink. Politely, Des and I thanked them but declined the offer – conscious that having members of the media present at such a sensitive time for the family might appear intrusive. About ten minutes later, another member of the family exited the house and issued a second invitation. As we were about to decline, she pointed out that if we didn't come up to the warmth of the house, Sophie's frail, elderly mother would insist on bringing a cup of tea down to us.

Embarrassed, we accepted the offer and walked up to the house, being immediately ushered to a seat by the fire that crackled in the traditional-style hearth that Sophie had kept when she first bought the house. Tea and coffee was poured, French cheese was produced and Georges and Marguerite endeavoured to make us feel welcome despite the fact I have only rusty French and many of those present did not speak English. When Des and I eventually left the house some thirty minutes later, we could not escape the question as to why such terrible things seem to happen to truly decent people.

Twelve years earlier at this precise time, Sophie Toscan du Plantier fled her west Cork holiday home – overlooking the Schull–Goleen countryside with the loom of the Fastnet lighthouse in the distance – in a doomed bid to save herself. Her only hope was that her attacker would panic and flee. Then she could either hide in the lonely mountain fields or else stumble on until she found help. But her attacker did neither. Sophie simply had nowhere to run to.

The killer remorselessly chased the 39-year-old French woman as she tried desperately to scramble to safety in the darkness. Sophie ultimately made it less than 100 metres before the assailant caught the terrified woman at the bottom of the hill directly below her holiday home. More than likely, her killer used the lights from her own home to help track her down in the darkness.

Gardaí later speculated that Sophie – racing in the darkness – had got her clothing snagged on a barbed-wire fence near the iron gate that guards the boreen to her home.

Sophie was wearing a white 'nightie' T-shirt, white cotton leggings and a navy-blue dressing gown. Her leggings had a patch torn from them – and a snag of clothing was later found by Gardaí on barbed wire nearby. It provided the only delay her killer needed and, with a savage series of blows to the head, knocked Sophie to the ground. If the French mother of one had screamed for help to the lonely hills that surround Toormore, no one heard her. Yet, almost two decades on from the brutal murder, Sophie's screams for justice are still echoing around the haunting west Cork landscape she loved so much.

What is perhaps the most heart-rending aspect of the brutal killing on 23 December 1996 is that, but for a series of coincidences, Sophie might never have been at Toormore to be attacked. She had been scheduled to fly back to France from Cork Airport on 23 December to spend Christmas with her family and then New Year with her husband, Daniel, in Dakar in Africa. But she had tried to fly back twenty-four hours early and had been unable to get a flight from Cork Airport because of the traditional Christmas bookings rush. Sophie spent her last night at Toormore reading poetry and phoning friends back in France. The last phone call she made was to her husband, Daniel, in Paris. In an eerie coincidence, Gardaí found the book of William Butler Yeats poetry that

Sophie was reading open at the page showing 'Dreams of Death'.

When she was attacked at her holiday home, she had been unable to flee uphill – apparently blocked both by her killer and a high embankment – to the only people who could potentially have helped her, Shirley Foster and Alfie Lyons. Sophie's neighbours heard nothing that terrible night – their home was simply too far away. The 39-year-old's body was eventually discovered by Shirley Foster as she drove carefully downhill on the morning of 23 December going to Schull to do some final bits of Christmas shopping. In an interview in 2010 with one of France's top current affairs programmes, *Sept à Huit* on TF1, Shirley said she would never forget the terrible discovery that morning. 'I drove my car down here – there used to be a lot more bushes. So I could not see anything. I would not have been able to see anything at all until I arrived at this corner. She [Sophie] was lying here inside the gate with her head here and her feet down there. I saw she was lying on her back with her right shoulder covered in streaks of blood.'

Sophie Toscan du Plantier had fallen in love with the wild, rugged and desolate landscape of west Cork on her first visit in 1991 and determined to buy a holiday home locally. She visited numerous properties with a friend in 1992 before finally settling on Toormore. Isolated and lonely, Toormore boasted unparalleled tranquillity and panoramic views over the west Cork coastline all the way to the Fastnet Rock and its evocative lighthouse. Sophie purchased Toormore in January 1993 and, for four years, came for annual holidays with her family, her friends and her son, Pierre-Louis Bauday, a child by her first marriage. Often she would come on her own to write prose and poetry, to think and to take walks along the windswept mountains and headlands.

Her particular loves were the rugged, lonely landscape around Brow Head, Mizen Head, Three Castles Head and Sheep's Head. Sophie would walk for hours, often stopping just to soak up the views and the sweeping seascapes in front of her. The scenery proved the inspiration for much of the poetry that she liked to write at Toormore, often by candlelight.

Marguerite Bouniol recalled that her daughter never seemed bothered by the house's isolation or any sense that she might be unsafe or in any danger. 'She loved it there. It was her special place,' she said. Over time, Sophie established her own routine – she would purchase cheese from American-born cheese-maker Bill Hogan, who operates an artisan facility almost at the foot of Mount Gabriel outside Schull, she would have lunch after a long morning walk at O'Sullivan's Pub in Crookhaven. She would chat with her housekeeper, Josephine Helen, or with a French couple who had relocated to west Cork, the Ungerers. She would go to Goleen or Schull to shop – often to pick up local crafts or food produce to bring back as gifts to friends in France. At Toormore, she would always sit and write either in an upstairs window facing out towards the Fastnet or on an outside bench, again facing towards the wild and rugged coast.

The first Gardaí at the murder scene quickly realised that Sophie had met a horrific death. Extreme, almost cruel violence had been visited upon the petite woman. A later post mortem examination would find that she died from severe head injuries. Her right cheekbone was fractured and partially crushed. Her bottom lip and gums were ripped. Her eye socket was shattered. In her desperate attempts to protect herself Sophie had tried to shield her face and head with her hands. The injuries testified to this fact. Her left hand was fractured and there were also fractures to the fingers on both her hands. There were deep scratches and blood streaks on her right hip, her left forearm and her stomach. Ten separate cuts were counted on her scalp and head. Even more appallingly, traces of a boot mark were found on her neck, as if her killer had stamped on her.

The murder probe that followed was one of the biggest ever mounted by Gardaí. But, over the course of fifteen years, no one was ever charged with the crime let alone brought to trial. The Garda murder file was one of the largest and most detailed ever prepared in the history of the force. But the DPP did not sanction a court charge. For Sophie's family, hope quickly turned to frustration at the delays within the Irish judicial system. It became a period of rapidly increasing frustration and disillusionment for the du Plantier and Bouniol families and Sophie's friends.

From 1997, Georges and Marguerite Bouniol began making the annual trip to Toormore to mark the anniversary of their daughter's death. They were usually accompanied by Sophie's aunt, Marie-Madeline Opalka, and were provided with a translator by the French embassy in Ireland and a liaison officer by the Gardaí. The group established a routine whereby they would stay in the Toormore house – which was now owned by Sophie's son, Pierre-Louis – and lay a wreath of lilies at the simple Celtic stone cross that marks the spot where her body was found. The cross is simply inscribed 'Sophie' and everyone who travels to the house passes directly by the monument. The family would then attend a special anniversary Mass in Goleen Church, usually celebrated by Parish Priest Fr John O'Donovan.

For Marguerite and Georges, the kindness of west Cork locals towards them was matched by the sympathy and support of Gardaí. Yet all the sympathy and kindness could not eradicate their frustration at the fact Sophie's killer or killers were still walking free as the months turned to years after their daughter's death. 'The policemen we met are very kind people – they always kept us informed as much as they could,' Marguerite said. 'But I have to say that I could not understand the way that the Anglo-Saxon judiciary system was working.

'We come back to west Cork every year [for the anniversaries]. But it is very, very difficult for us. We hope and we pray that justice will be done some day. She [Sophie] was viciously killed – her face was smashed. But we can do absolutely nothing. We can do nothing for her except fight for justice. She has been murdered in terrible circumstances – and the fact that she was left like that. It is terrible. Would you do it to a dog?' she asked.

Sophie's husband, Daniel du Plantier, made just a single trip to west Cork following his wife's murder and before his own untimely death in March 2003 while attending a film industry function in Germany. Daniel had vowed to the French media that he would never visit Ireland until someone was charged with his wife's killing. But he decided to visit west Cork on 7 July 2000 when it was obvious there were serious problems with a potential prosecution in Ireland and after Sophie's mother appealed to him. Having flown into Cork Airport, he was briefed by senior Gardaí at Bandon Garda Station before he staged a special press conference in the then Jury's Hotel on the Western Road in Cork city. Daniel du Plantier – a film producer with powerful connections within French political and cultural circles – was accompanied by his lawyer, Paul Haennig, Sophie's son, Pierre-Louis, his own son, Davide du Plantier and the French Consul in Cork, Françoise Letellier.

I attended the press conference that day and it was immediately clear that Daniel du Plantier knew more than he was prepared to say to the media, which had followed his every move over the course of forty-eight hours. The press conference was held in a business room in the hotel (since demolished, although a new hotel has been built on the site) and was packed with reporters and photographers from every Irish newspaper, as well as reporters from newspapers and radio stations in Britain and France.

Daniel du Plantier was visibly frustrated that no one was before the Irish courts and, at times, struggled to contain that frustration. He renewed his appeal for anyone with information about Sophie's death to come forward – but he was blunt when I asked him whether he believed the police knew the identity of the individual or individuals who had killed his wife. 'Yes, I believe they do.' Mr du Plantier was also adamant that, had the 1996 murder occurred in France, the killer would already be several years into his prison term.

While Mr du Plantier was courteous and diplomatic to journalists at the press conference, it was obvious he was far from happy with how his wife's murder probe was progressing. 'You get [them] but you cannot do anything. It is a joke? No, it is not a joke – it is the law. The habeas corpus system is a better system to protect the human being. But the system also protects the killer of my wife,' he said. 'They [the Gardaí] know 90 per cent or more. But it is like a painting – somewhere you could have little images you could miss.'

His final words at the press conference underlined just how much west Cork meant to his wife. 'It was the place Sophie loved above all else in the world. It was as if Sophie was behind every door [at Toormore],' he added. Yet, ultimately, Daniel's visit changed very little and a prosecution seemed no nearer.

Two years earlier, in February 1998, Mr du Plantier had launched a stinging attack against the Irish authorities in a French newspaper interview over the way in which the entire murder was handled. 'The Irish told us nothing – not a word, nothing,' he told *Le Figaro*. 'In the neighbourhood, everyone knew who she was even if I went there only once, at her request.' He added that he remained concerned that Sophie's killing might have had a sexual motivation even if there was no post mortem indication of such an attack. 'It could have played a part at the start. There could have been the desire to seduce a woman – to take her. [But] she refuses – she fights. It turns ugly. She was hit in the head savagely. But I don't think the crime was premeditated,' he added.

Daniel du Plantier did not live to see the next major development in the case – a high-profile libel trial in December 2003. He died from a massive heart attack while attending the Berlin Film Festival in 2003. Had he lived, Daniel du

Plantier would undoubtedly have been as transfixed as the rest of Ireland by the dramatic revelations in Cork Circuit Civil Court.

The libel case was taken by a Schull-based freelance journalist, Ian Bailey. The Manchester-born reporter – who had relocated to west Cork in 1991 – sued eight British and Irish newspapers over their coverage of the Sophie Toscan du Plantier murder. He claimed he had effectively been branded as the killer – and had been left living a nightmare existence in west Cork as a result. His counsel, Jim Duggan BL, claimed the net result of the coverage was that Ian Bailey was 'shunned, persecuted and victimised'. 'Within his own community he is referred to as the murderer,' said Duggan. Ian Bailey himself claimed that the newspaper coverage of the murder investigation had left him 'to some degree untouchable. Life has been a struggle – it feels like I am being eaten alive. I have been battered.'

Ian Bailey was born in Manchester in 1957. He came from a middle-class background and went on to attend Gloucester Grammar School. English was his favourite subject and he eventually settled on a career in journalism. He initially worked for a freelance agency in Gloucester for five years before relocating to Cheltenham where he opened up his own agency. It was a reasonably successful move and Bailey's work appeared in a range of British publications ranging from *The Daily Telegraph* to the *Daily Mail* and the *Daily Mirror*. He also did work for the BBC and HTV-Wales.

However, by the late 1980s and early 1990s Ian Bailey had become tired of life in England. His marriage to fellow journalist Sara Limbrick had ended in divorce and he was suddenly fed up of the daily grind of running a freelance agency. Like many Englishmen before him, he settled on starting a new life in Ireland. After a brief period in Wicklow, he decided to base himself in the Schull area of west Cork. In the early 1990s, west Cork had become a magnet for people from the UK, France, Germany, Holland and even the United States seeking a new life. It was also given an internationally high profile following the decision of luminaries – including Disney heir, Roy Disney, Academy award winning producer, Sir David Puttnam, and Academy Award winning actor, Jeremy Irons – to relocate to the area.

Ian Bailey initially worked in a fish factory where he met Welsh-born artist Jules Thomas, when she called to purchase some fresh fish. Ian Bailey eventually rented a flat from her for a short period after they began a relationship in 1992, before moving in to her house just a few miles west of Schull. Ms Thomas was a successful painter and shared common interests with Ian Bailey, including music and organic gardening. 'We fell in love,' Ian Bailey later explained.

Ian Bailey worked as a gardener-cum-handyman in the Schull area, eventually becoming dubbed a 'New Age' gardener for his dedication to organic produce and his use of natural materials in his garden designs. He also fell in love with Irish culture, learning to play the bodhrán and, for a time, even referring to himself by the Gaelic form of his name, Eoin O'Baille. However, by 1995 he had decided to try to resurrect his career as freelance journalist in order to provide a potentially valuable additional source of income.

He had himself reported on Sophie's murder in December 1996 and January 1997. His work had appeared in several

Irish, British and French newspapers. For a time, Ian Bailey's work was in enormous demand. By late January, however, other reporters became aware that Gardaí were taking an increasing interest in him. But it was still a sensation when Ian Bailey was arrested by Gardaí on 10 February 1997. He was released without charge only to be greeted by a media scrum outside the home he shared with his partner. Nearly a year later, on 27 January 1998, Ian Bailey was arrested again for further questioning in relation to Sophie's death. As on the first occasion, he was released without charge.

In his two-week libel hearing in 2003, Mr Bailey claimed that sinister attempts were being made to frame him for the crime. He accused Gardaí of having threatened him – and claimed one Garda warned him that he could be 'found with a bullet in the back of his head'. He alleged that another Garda had insisted he was 'a werewolf monster' capable of such appalling acts during a full moon. Ian Bailey insisted that he had never met Sophie Toscan du Plantier and that he only ever saw her once when she was pointed out to him in 1995 through the window of a neighbour's house when she was several hundred metres away.

The newspapers were represented by Senior Counsel Paul Gallagher who would, just five years later, be appointed Ireland's Attorney General. In a dramatic move, the defence applied for access to key elements of the State file on Sophie's death. The State – while not a direct party to the libel case – objected to any Gardaí directly involved in the murder case being called to offer evidence. After legal argument, the trial justice, Judge Patrick Moran, granted the defence application.

Ian Bailey's own diaries – which had been seized by the

Gardaí as part of their probe – were now to be introduced as evidence by the defendants. They painted a picture of a man deeply ashamed of his occasional outbursts of violence against his partner (Jules Thomas) and who was fixated with issues relating to alcohol, sex and drugs. In one memorable passage, he described himself as 'a crow'; in another, following a violent confrontation with his partner, he wrote: 'One act of whiskey-induced madness – coupled and cracked – and in an act of awful violence I severely damaged you and made you feel that death was near. As I lay and write, I know there is something badly wrong with me. For through remorse filled sentiments, disgust fills me. I am afraid for myself – a cowardly fear. In doing what I did I am damned to hell.'

The two-week hearing and its dramatic revelations caused a national sensation. The trial opened with a half-page of coverage in most national papers. By the time it finished, it was front-page news with two full pages of colour and analysis inside. The hearing was receiving blanket coverage on Irish radio and television – and, by the time it concluded, was even featuring on UK and French stations.

The hearing revolved around several key issues: Ian Bailey insisted he did not know and had never met Sophie Toscan du Plantier. He also insisted he was being unfairly branded over the crime. But several witnesses – Malachi Reed, Ritchie and Rosie Shelly – offered dramatic testimony of how Ian Bailey had effectively linked himself to the crime through comments made to them. The Shellys – who had attended a New Year's Eve party in 1998 in Ian Bailey's home with Jules Thomas – were so unnerved by his behaviour they insisted on leaving. Malachi Reed – who, as a fourteen-year-old schoolboy, had accepted a lift from Ian Bailey – claimed he turned to him and said: 'It was fine up until I went up and bashed her f***ing brains in.'

In all cases, Mr Bailey insisted that he was merely repeating rumours he had heard locally about himself. He vehemently denied that any of the comments were confessions and his barrister dismissed some of the statements as mere 'rubbish'.

Yet arguably the highest-profile witness in the libel hearing was former Schull shopkeeper, Marie Farrell. In dramatic testimony, she told the Circuit Court that she had been living in fear of Ian Bailey. Central to Mrs Farrell's testimony was the claim that she had seen a tall man wearing a dark coat and walking, swinging his arms in distinctive fashion, in the early hours of 23 December 1996 not far from Sophie Toscan du Plantier's home. That man was later identified to her as Ian Bailey and she informed the Gardaí of what she had seen.

On its own, this claim was sensational because Ian Bailey had steadfastly maintained that he had never left the home he shared with Jules Thomas on the late evening of 22 December or early hours of 23 December. In later testimony, Mrs Farrell claimed that Ian Bailey had tried to persuade her to make a statement claiming that Gardaí were putting her under duress to make a false statement. She denied this – and in cross-examination insisted she was not being put under any duress by detectives about what she had seen on the Schull–Goleen road on 23 December.

Ultimately, the libel hearing heard twenty independent witnesses offer evidence with most partly or fully contradicting evidence offered by Ian Bailey. In contrast, Ian Bailey said of the Reed/Shelly incidents that he was merely repeating what was being said about him in the community. In the case of the Shellys, he said he could understand how a misunderstanding might have arisen.

Judge Patrick Moran ultimately ruled in favour of six of the eight newspapers – with Ian Bailey awarded damages of just €8,000 against the *Irish Sun* and the *Irish Mirror*. But the legal costs estimated to be facing Mr Bailey in relation to the cases he lost were in excess of €200,000. The ruling – and the cost implications – sparked an avalanche of media reports on Ian Bailey and the Sophie Toscan du Plantier case. Ian Bailey, for his part, confirmed he would appeal to the High Court.

In France, Sophie's family thought that finally something was going to happen in a judicial context in Ireland. But they were wrong. Despite the exhaustive coverage of the libel hearing and Garda hopes that new evidence might come to light as a result, nothing happened. The family signalled their intention now to take a civil action arising from Sophie's death – but this was dramatically stalled when, just two years later, the case was marked by a spectacular new twist.

In October 2005, Marie Farrell bizarrely retracted the statement about Ian Bailey she had made to Gardaí – and claimed she had only made the statement after being pressurised by Gardaí. Critically, this meant that her evidence to the libel hearing was now also being called into question.

Ian Bailey immediately paid tribute to the courage of Mrs Farrell in coming forward and said it vindicated the position he had consistently maintained that he was an innocent man being wrongly targeted. In a statement issued through his Cork solicitor, Frank Buttimer, Mr Bailey said Mrs Farrell's retraction of the claims she had made about him was hugely important. It emerged that Marie Farrell had contacted Mr Bailey's solicitor, outlined her position and then voluntarily agreed to clarify her position. Mr Bailey's solicitor had also advised her to take legal advice.

'Mr Bailey is greatly relieved at this development – he is grateful to Mrs Farrell for her courage, and I genuinely mean that, her courage in coming forward at this point in time and being satisfied to correct the wrong that she could be accused of doing,' Mr Buttimer said. 'The easier option [for her] would have been to remain silent and allow the thing to stay as it was and fester. She has now put herself back into the focus and the spotlight. I think this was the first of the seriously incriminating statements. It is abundantly clear to me that it was based on her statement that the arrest occurred.'

The stunning turn of events sparked an immediate Garda investigation into what had happened, with the probe being led by Assistant Commissioner Ray McAndrew. In the wake of the startling developments in Ireland, Sophie's family felt they had no option but to halt their plans for a civil action. Ian Bailey also pressed ahead with his legal action for the return of possessions seized from him by Gardaí in 1997 and 1998. Ultimately, this action in the District Court would lead to the clearest indication yet that there were no plans in Ireland for any action arising from Sophie Toscan du Plantier's death.

Ian Bailey's High Court libel appeal finally opened on 13 February 2007. It lasted just one week before collapsing spectacularly – which was surprising at the time but, in hindsight, was perfectly in keeping with a case that had more twists and turns than a James Bond film. Ian Bailey was not paid a euro in damages although the six newspapers did agree to make a contribution towards his legal costs. A statement agreed by both sides was then read out with Mr Bailey later indicating that he intended to sue the State over his treatment.

Yet what was most significant about the Circuit Court civil case in 2003 and the High Court case in 2007 was that elements of the Garda murder investigation, which would ordinarily never have been publicised, suddenly came to light. Sophie's family learned facts and details that they had never heard before and witnesses painted a picture of the events in west Cork in 1995–1996. But the family also learned that there was now no chance of a prosecution in Ireland unless Gardaí received new information and evidence.

The reality was that the case was hugely problematic from the start for the DPP. There were mistakes from the very beginning. There was a crucial delay in getting a pathologist to the scene in December 1996, which affected the possibility of pinpointing the precise time of Sophie's fatal attack. Elements of the extended crime scene were not comprehensively preserved due to the location of the murder beside the main access road for residents. Detectives were further frustrated by the lack of witnesses to the crime and the inability to locate the murder weapon itself. A further blow – arguably the most telling blow to the entire investigation – came with the failure of forensic tests, including fingerprinting and DNA analysis, to yield any breakthrough clues as to the identity of the killer. Detectives had initially hoped that material recovered from under Sophie's fingernails would deliver vital clues to the killer's identity. But the only identifiable DNA was that of Sophie herself.

To this day, senior detectives remain amazed that such a

violent attack left no tell-tale forensic clue as to the identity of the killer. Even more bizarrely, detectives are convinced that whoever killed Sophie must have left the scene covered in blood. They are convinced that that person would have found it virtually impossible to clean themselves up without someone else spotting the blood or becoming suspicious. Yet no one ever came forward.

Sophie's uncle, Jean-Pierre Gazeau, explained that the disappointment experienced by the family since 1996 has been overwhelming. 'After all those years, we had the feeling that everything was blocked – completely helpless. We have tried to move things forward and we are very happy that, over recent years, they have made some good progress. There is only one message from us – the person or persons who committed this terrible act, if they want to help us, they must come forward. This is the only message we can give.'

For Sophie's mother, there is now the all-pervading fear that she may die without knowing that the person responsible for her daughter's death has been brought to justice. 'That is my fear – it is my fear every day. I have always feared that I may die before knowing the whole truth about Sophie's murder and I still do,' she said. Marguerite keeps a framed photo of Sophie by her bed in her Paris apartment. 'It is a photo of Sophie at work – it is a photo I always keep next to me.'

Sophie's son, Pierre-Louis, echoed the frustration expressed by Daniel du Plantier in 2000. Pierre-Louis – who accompanied the French film executive on that trip to west Cork – kept his thoughts private until, in a French TV interview in June 2004, his calm finally shattered and he lashed out at the Irish judicial system.

'We do not understand how, after seven years, a man can be at his home, quiet, go in the village, shop there, meet people there, when there are such accusations.' he said. 'I was only fifteen years old when this happened. I have tried to stay away from this story. In the meantime, my grandmother [Marguerite Bouniol] and my family were struggling to find the secret behind this mystery. Now, I am eager to speak – to speak of my bitterness with Irish justice, which is now going around in circles. In France, such a man would have been in detention,' he declared.

Ultimately, Pierre-Louis's comments in 2004 would have reverberations in later years. By 2007, the Garda murder file remained open and active in Ireland – but the DPP had not sanctioned a prosecution. Privately, both Gardaí and legal experts acknowledged that, without crucial new evidence or witnesses, there would now never be a prosecution in Ireland.

That triggered a response in France where Sophie's family and friends decided to change tactics. If they could not secure a prosecution in Ireland, they would use one of the procedures of Napoleonic law to press for a prosecution in France. The Sophie Toscan du Plantier Truth Association (STDPTA) was founded in October 2007 and began to forge strong links with Irish victim support groups. Within months, the STDPTA had garnered the support of powerful figures in France. The late Daniel du Plantier was one of the most influential figures in French cinema and a friend of former President Jacques Chirac. The STDPTA was now openly endorsed by Gilles Jacob, President of the Cannes Film Festival, and Jacques Toubon, a former French justice minister.

Events gathered pace when the French appointed a

Paris-based magistrate to conduct a fresh probe into Sophie's murder. Patrick Gachon moved quickly and sought access to key information in Ireland regarding the Garda investigation. He was soon assisted by a second magistrate, Nathalie Dutarte. By 2008, the Irish government and Gardaí had agreed to provide the French with access to the murder file – in itself a tacit admission that a prosecution would now never occur in Ireland. The French also received the full post mortem examination report conducted by the then State Pathologist, Dr John Harbison.

The magistrate wasted no time and, in June 2008, signalled his intention to exhume Sophie's body for a fresh post mortem examination in France. The exhumation was conducted on 1 July and a whole new battery of high-tech DNA fingerprint tests were ordered, although none, ultimately, yielded new evidence. In June 2009, Magistrates Gachon and Dutarte arrived in west Cork to examine the murder scene for themselves and to meet with senior Gardaí. On 19 October 2009, two Gardaí – Superintendent Liam Horgan and Detective Sergeant Fitzgerald – flew to Paris to be formally interviewed as part of the new French probe.

But the French then caused a sensation when, on 7 April 2010, they issued a European Arrest Warrant for Ian Bailey. The EAW was passed to the Department of Justice in Dublin and, on 23 April, the High Court endorsed the EAW. Ian Bailey was arrested by Gardaí from the Dublin-based Extradition Unit at his Schull home shortly before midnight. After being kept overnight at Bandon Garda Station he was taken to Dublin to appear before the High Court. He was released on bail after a special sitting of the High Court the following day (24 April) and his legal team confirmed that the French extradition request would be vigorously contested – potentially to the Supreme Court and, if necessary, the European Court of Justice itself. Ian Bailey was excused a personal attendance at the next two High Court hearings because he was sitting his final year law exams at University College Cork (UCC).

The extradition case represented a landmark in Irish law because, to date, no one has ever been extradited from Ireland for questioning or trial in a foreign jurisdiction for an offence that happened here. Pointedly, Ian Bailey had never been charged with any offence whatsoever related to Sophie Toscan du Plantier in Ireland. Ian Bailey's solicitor, Frank Buttimer, described the French extradition request as 'extraordinary' and 'a nonsense'.

'Mr Bailey has always protested and maintained his innocence. With every due respect and sympathy for the family of the late Mme Toscan du Plantier, he has always maintained that any effort by the police to implicate him in relation to the unlawful killing of Mme Toscan du Plantier was [both] misguided and corrupt,' Mr Buttimer said. Mr Bailey's partner, Jules Thomas, warned one French reporter that: 'They are still making a big mistake.'

It also marked a marathon legal process that both sides seemed determined to fight through every possible judicial avenue. If the French thought the Irish judicial system would deliver a rapid verdict on their extradition request, they were to be sorely disappointed. Two months after Ian Bailey first appeared before the High Court, the STDPTA issued a statement querying how long the process would actually take.

On 8 June 2010, STDPTA President Jean-Pierre Gazeau said the lobby group now had concerns over the Irish judicial move. 'The Association is surprised by the additional time given to Ian Bailey, to prepare its components of argument against the simple fact of being heard by the French Judiciary,' he said.

'The Association expects that this additional time, provided for by European legislation, be utilised in a spirit of cooperation, by the Irish and French judiciary to enhance conditions in establishing and disclosing the truth. The family of Sophie Toscan du Plantier, their friends, like all justice-loving people, would have difficulty in accepting, fourteen years after the heinous assassination, any manoeuvres or tactics which would cause unjustified delays or submerge proceedings,' he added.

The high-profile yet convoluted legal battle has left Sophie's family facing a roller-coaster of emotions despite the number of years that have passed since the murder. Stoically, Sophie's parents and aunt have refused to indulge in point-scoring against the Irish judicial system over the failure to charge anyone with the killing – while quietly hoping that the French judicial process will provide them with answers to the questions that have haunted them since 1996.

'Regarding the Irish legal system, it is not a question of judging it. But, for us, who are accustomed to the Latin [Napoleonic] legal system, we are surprised by some of the Irish procedures or rather non-decisions to initiate those procedures,' Marguerite explained. 'What is the [past] concern is the absence of cooperation between the two states, France and Ireland, who have not worked together in the past and who have not made one iota of progress in the area of legal cooperation. The death of Sophie did not even serve to advance such cooperation [until now].

'We are very, very disappointed but also very angry that things have not advanced. We are traumatised. After all these years, the sadness is still there. We would like her [Sophie] to be beside us. We would like her to be there – to give her a hug. But we cannot. It is despair,' she added.

Sophie's aunt, Marie-Madeline Opalka, has never given up hope that someday someone will answer for what was done to Sophie. Her constant appeals for help and information on behalf of the Gardaí in west Cork were as touching as they were heartfelt. In 2006, she addressed Mass-goers outside Goleen Church. 'I want to tell you what the old Pope, John Paul II, said – do not be afraid. If you know something, please tell the police. They did [everything] perfectly – but not only that, they were always, always supporting us. We never arrived in Cork in this terrible moment without members of the police being there to help us. And for that I want to thank them all very, very much.'

But it is the words of her sister, Marguerite, that are most poignant. Sophie's mother vowed that, despite ill-health and the time elapsed since her daughter's death, she will never stop campaigning for the truth about what happened that dark night of 22–23 December 1996.

'I have had to be twice as strong as anyone. But it is natural, is it not, that I should want my daughter's murderer to be behind bars? There are moments I do not believe at all. There is something totally unjust and abnormal about parents surviving their children,' she said. 'I know you will say I am biased because I was her mother, but Sophie really did have all the qualities – she loved life, she was gay and pretty. She loved meeting people and loved nature. She spoke to everyone. In Ireland, the people we met told us: "She was like one of us." But [after all this time] it is still very difficult to talk about.'

On Wednesday 15 December 2010, Sophie's parents and aunt flew into Cork for a ceremony in Toormore and Goleen the following weekend to mark the fourteenth anniversary of their daughter's death. Coincidentally, the following day (16 December) the extradition hearing involving Ian Bailey finally opened before the High Court in Dublin. Ten days earlier, Mr Bailey had graduated with an honours BCL law degree from UCC.

Marguerite Bouniol told the author that the family were not in Ireland because of the extradition case. 'We are old now so we will not suffer for many years more. We do not wish what we are living for anyone – we suffer a lot. We do not come here [to Ireland] for what will happen tomorrow [in the High Court]. That is not our problem. We do not come for that. This is the job of the justice system.

'We could not come [to Ireland] last year but we are happy to come back this year because we owe it to our daughter. She suffered so much when she tried to escape and then she was hunted down. She suffered so much that we want to suffer as well,' she said.

In the High Court, Mr Bailey's legal team explained over the two-day hearing (16 and 17 December) that there was absolutely 'no evidence' to support the French extradition bid and they accused the Paris authorities of playing a game of 'cat and mouse' with the 53-year-old. The Court was also told that Mr Bailey had been deeply traumatised by the ongoing focus on him. The extradition bid was, his legal team complained, effectively the use of the judicial process to torture Mr Bailey.

The Court reserved judgement in the case until early 2011 but, irrespective of the ruling, it appeared almost certain that the case would be appealed to the Supreme Court. There is also the likelihood that the case could ultimately be referred to the European Court given the landmark legal issues involved.

9

Pawel Kalite & Mariusz Szwajkos

'They only came to Ireland to build a new life'

The sentencing hearing did little to quell the obvious anger coursing through David Curran's young veins. The 19-year-old – nicknamed 'Schillaci' to his teenage friends in Dublin's Drimnagh suburb in honour of the Italian football star of the Italia '90 World Cup Finals – did not appear chastened by his appearance before the Central Criminal Court in the plush new Criminal Courts complex at Parkgate Street in Dublin.

The prospect of two mandatory life sentences would have

reduced most other people to trembling, sobbing wrecks. But the anger that coursed deep within David Curran was all too evident as he first snarled at a youth worker attempting to help him and then glared at some of his supporters in the main public gallery of the court. Despite the fact that it was May 2010, two years and three months since he had driven a screwdriver into the brains of two young Polish men, killing them both, the full import of what David Curran had done still did not seem to have fully registered with him.

The events of that terrible day of 23 February 2008 on Drimnagh's Benbulbin Road fixed an alarming spotlight on the chaotic lifestyle being led by some Irish teens – and the manner in which alcohol and drugs were inextricably linked with acts of ferocious violence. The case also sparked myriad questions about drug and alcohol abuse within society, the integration of East European migrants into Irish communities and the total lack of provocation now required for some appalling attacks of violence.

As he was later being led away to commence the two life terms imposed on him by Mr Justice Liam McKechnie, Curran of Lissadel Green, Drimnagh, briefly smiled back at the court and emitted a short, sharp laugh. It was behaviour that, to some, appeared to be in stark contrast to the fulsome apology just issued on his behalf by his defence counsel, Giollaoisa Ó Lideadha SC, to the families of his two Polish victims, Pawel Kalite (twenty-nine) from Świętokrzyskie and Mariusz Szwajkos (twenty-seven) from Szczucin.

It was also in stark contrast to his reaction to his initial conviction on the double-murder charge by the Central Criminal Court jury just twenty-four hours earlier. Curran had been convicted following five hours and forty-five minutes of deliberations by the jury. He was convicted of Pawel Kalite's murder by unanimous decision and of Mariusz Szwajkos' murder by an 11–1 majority verdict. As he awaited the verdicts, Curran had seemed unable to sit still in the courtroom – fidgeting, glancing around and shuffling around in his seat.

But when the verdicts were eventually read out, Curran placed his head in his hands and held it there for several seconds. When he finally raised his head to glance around the courtroom, tears were slowly streaming down his face. His co-accused, Sean Keogh (twenty-one), was acquitted by the jury of the double murder. Keogh of Vincent Street West, Inchicore, Dublin, had earlier pleaded guilty to assault causing harm to Pawel Kalite. This involved kicking the Polish man in the head as he fell to the ground after being stabbed in the temple by David Curran. Sean Keogh's defence counsel, Patrick Gageby SC, acknowledged to the court that Keogh's act had been 'an appalling thing' – but that his client had never touched Mariusz Szwajkos. Furthermore, he said, he was never the instigator in the terrible proceedings that night in the South Dublin suburb.

Curran had admitted manslaughter but denied the double murder, claiming provocation. He insisted his actions were underpinned by his consumption of alcohol and drugs earlier that evening – and that he was also in an emotional state because he had heard that his own father had been stabbed. He claimed he had only gone up to the fast-food takeaway at the centre of the Benbulbin Road confrontation because he wanted to find those responsible for allegedly hurting his father. In fact, his father had not been stabbed or harmed in any way – and Pawel Kalite was merely going home with his food when he got into a verbal row with another youth, an unnamed fifteen-year-old.

This youth, the court was told, was 'the engine' behind the tragedy of the evening – along with a teenage girl who seemed to help light the emotional fuses. The unnamed fifteen-year-old had got into a verbal row with one of the Polish men after apparently bumping into him as he left the takeway. Pawel challenged the boy, angry at his behaviour and lack of apology.

An older man at the scene, who knew the fifteen-year-old, intervened and told the Pole: 'He is only a young fella – leave him alone.' Two teenage girls who also happened to be nearby got involved and the incident suddenly and dramatically escalated. Pawel Kalite was attacked by unnamed teens and, as the State's opening of the case outlined: 'He [Pawel] got a bit of a beating.'

Pawel was subsequently knocked to the ground before being able to regain his feet and stagger off to the house he shared with his friend, Mariusz Szwajkos. But even as he limped home, Pawel was further jeered by a group of teens who had gathered at the scene when they realised there had been trouble. Pawel was very upset over how he had been treated and publicly insulted. The older man left the scene and advised the teens to go home as well.

However, one of the teenage girls then used a mobile phone to contact David Curran. When informed of what had just happened – and the false claim that his father had been injured – Curran and his friend Sean Keogh arrived at the scene 'full of fight'. Curran's immediate reaction on arriving at the scene was incendiary – and at one point he even launched a ferocious attack on a parked car that he mistakenly thought contained the two Polish men.

An eyewitness offered stark testimony to a hushed Central Criminal Court about what happened that evening. Treacy Dillon was standing on Benbulbin Road when she saw the initial confrontation between the fifteen-year-old teen and Pawel Kalite. 'The lad in the grey tracksuit, the two young girls and this older man were basically killing the bald chap on the ground. They were kicking him.' Later, the group dispersed and the older man took the young boy away. 'One of the girls was carrying a bottle of vodka and the other had what appeared to be a bottle of wine.' As a bruised Pawel Kalite walked by them, one of the teenage girls struck him. 'One of them gave him a clatter across the face, across the neck. [But] he just crossed the road.'

The group then dispersed towards a nearby pub only to recongregate when David Curran and Sean Keogh arrived on the scene. 'There was a tall lad wearing a black and red jacket. I seen a screwdriver in his hand. They were screaming: "Where's the bastard? I am going to kill him. Where is the c**t?" I rang the police on my mobile – you just kind of knew what was going to happen,' Treacy Dillon added. Just minutes later, as she returned to her home just ten houses away from where the Polish men lived, Ms Dillon spotted two bodies – one of whom was on the footpath with his face lying on a step. It was the bald man she had spotted earlier at the chipper.

Another eyewitness, Darren Lee, said he saw a bald man – Pawel Kalite – struggle to get off the ground after the

Benbulbin Road attack and then be jeered by the group of teenage girls. 'They [the girls] walked over toward the baldy guy. I heard a bottle smash off the ground. One of the girls had a bottle – I went inside to ring the Gardaí because I thought there was going to be an incident.'

Minutes later, an older teenager arrived at the scene and started kicking a parked car and screaming: "Was it youse? Who did it?" Local landlord Rory O'Connor was so concerned by what was happening on the street that he ran inside his property to get his car keys so he could offer the assault victim a lift home for his own safety. 'I just sensed there was going to be trouble,' he told the court. But, despite driving up Benbulbin Road in a courageous attempt to help, Mr O'Connor could not locate the bald man who had just been attacked.

The fatal attacks themselves were nothing short of horrific. Pawel made it home only for the group containing David Curran and Sean Keogh to arrive screaming outside his house a few minutes later. Inside the house, Pawel met his friend Mariusz and two other Polish friends, Radek and Kamila Szeremeta. Pawel worked alongside Mariusz as a mechanic for Ace AutoBody on the Robin Hood Industrial Estate in Clondalkin. Pawel had a gash on his forehead and was visibly distressed. Kamila asked him what was wrong and he told her: 'I am almost thirty and those stupid little punks attacked me with a baseball bat.'

Her brother, Radek, had witnessed his friend being slapped by the teenage girls. Pawel was very upset and, as his Polish friends later told Gardaí, 'was so mad he was crying.' His friends were very concerned for him. Radek and Kamila

– on realising the teens were now outside the house – pleaded with Pawel not to go back outside. However, Pawel was so upset and indignant at what had been done to him he decided to face the teenagers. It was a fatal mistake.

Kamila stood on the path into their house with Pawel when the teenagers began roaring obscenities at them. '[They were] screaming and offending Polish people, saying: "All Polish are fuckers." [One of the teens] had a tool in his hand.' Kamila asked them why they were abusing Polish people when suddenly members of the group charged forward. 'He [one of the teens] was going for my head,' she explained. Kamila ducked under the swing of the heavy screwdriver which missed her by just a few inches – but Pawel Kalite collapsed seconds later after being struck in the side of the head with the heavy tool. His friend, Mariusz, immediately rushed out to his aid but was also struck in the head with the screwdriver.

Mariusz instantly collapsed to the ground, with his head heavily striking the pavement. 'You feel it [the impact] on the pavement,' Kamila told the trial. Her brother, Radek, emerged from the house to a scene of total horror with his two friends lying dying on the path, with blood everywhere. He told the trial that he heard one of the shocked teenage girls cry out: 'Oh my God, they killed him.'

A primary school student – who could not be named for legal reasons – also witnessed the fatal assault. 'I think David had a screwdriver and the Polish man tried to stop him. Then he stabbed him. I think in the side of the head,' she said. 'I think he [Mariusz] tried to jump over the wall to [help] his friend and I think he started fighting with David then. I think David stabbed the Polish fella then.'

Such were the appalling injuries sustained by the two Poles that neither had a realistic hope of survival. Post mortem examinations were conducted on both men by State Pathologist Dr Marie Cassidy. She found that both had died from deep, penetrative brain injuries inflicted by a cross-shaped or Phillips-type screwdriver. Pawel Kalite had two cross-shaped injuries on his left scalp – one of which penetrated the skull and left a gaping 11-centimetre-long wound, from left to right, through his brain. The internal structure of the brain was massively damaged and Dr Cassidy said, such was the scale of the injury, Mr Kalite was unlikely ever to have recovered. Mr Kalite had also suffered three broken teeth, multiple abrasions to his face, fractured ribs, a collapsed lung and a badly bruised arm.

Mariusz Szwajkos similarly had little chance of surviving the head wound he sustained. The stab wound to his head had penetrated his skull and left an 11-centimetre-long wound to his brain. In his case, this wound included damage to the brain stem, which was unrecoverable. 'He simply would not have recovered from the brain trauma,' Dr Cassidy said. Mariusz also had a fracture to the right side of his skull – possibly indicating that he was struck a blow to the head or struck his head off the pavement when falling. The post mortem revealed that his death was accelerated by the development of pneumonia while in hospital.

In stark evidence to the court, the young girl who had helped inflame tensions that night acknowledged that the group of teens was never going to walk away from the confrontation that evening once it had triggered. 'You wouldn't leave it if someone was after starting – nobody would.'

As the tears welled up in Curran's eyes as the murder convictions were returned, tears of a different sort were running down the face of Agnieszka Kalite. Justice had been done for her brother and she was weeping with relief that the family's ordeal was almost at an end. As her shoulders shook with the effort of subduing her sobs, a comforting arm was placed around her by Alan Kennedy, the man who had employed both her brother and Mariusz in Clondalkin. Twenty-four hours later, the trial concluded with two mandatory life sentences imposed on Curran.

Mr Ó Lideadha had told the Kalite and Szwajkos families that Curran was very sorry for what happened. Curran, he said, 'took full and exclusive criminal responsibility' for what had happened that awful February evening. The counsel also apologised on Curran's behalf to Sean Keogh, the young man who was his co-accused and who was acquitted by the jury on the murder charge. Curran was now sorry for having tried to implicate Keogh in the stabbings in the first place. At one point, Curran had claimed he had seen Keogh strike the fatal blows. He even told Gardaí that Keogh was not a friend but more of an enemy. Keogh, for his part, had insisted throughout to Gardaí that he had not stabbed anyone – but refused to identify the person who had wielded the screwdriver. 'I am no rat,' was all he would say.

The broad-brush apologies made little difference to the pain being endured by the Polish families of the two dead men. Pawel Kalite and Mariusz Szwajkos had only come to Ireland to make some money to build a better future for themselves in their native Poland. They liked Ireland, they were thrilled at the prospect of well-paid work and enjoyed the social life on offer in Dublin. They particularly liked and respected their employer, Alan Kennedy, who had always treated them fairly and well. But Poland, not Ireland, was their home and they dreamed of eventually saving enough to return to their birthplace to start their own businesses.

Instead, Pawel and Marius returned home in coffins. The double murder shocked not just the Irish nation but Poland itself where the killings generated banner headlines in the newspapers. Most of the stories focused on whether the double killing was motivated in any way by the fact the two victims were Polish. The killings also caused a seismic shock within Ireland's large Polish community. With more than 150,000 Poles living and working in Ireland, integration and cross-community relations had become an issue of paramount national importance. The double stabbing seemed to call into question everything that people had worked so hard and so long to achieve in terms of inter-community harmony and understanding.

As Mr Justice McKechnie would later declare, the killings were 'brutal, savage and could be described as sadistic'. Neither victim was left with any chance once the blow had been struck to his temple. The heavy weapon shattered the thin skull at the temple and plunged deep into their brains. Pawel died late on Wednesday night, five days after the savage attack. His friend Mariusz had died forty-eight hours earlier.

It was an attack that the Central Criminal Court heard had been carried out with 'lethal accuracy'. The case was shocking not just for the extreme, brutal violence exhibited by Curran following a relatively minor row outside a fast-food takeaway, but it was also shocking for the callous, almost dismissive attitude immediately adopted by the teen – and by the manner in which Curran, who had committed the stabbings, tried to blame his friend. Having stabbed both Polish men in the head, Curran ran from the scene as a young friend screamed at him: 'Come on, Schillaci – they're dead.'

Curran went home and had a curry for his dinner. One of the few redeeming features of the aftermath of the incident was that the teen's conscience apparently caused sufficient bother that he threw up in the toilet of a relative's house. A teenage girl who knew Curran and who was familiar with the tragic events of the evening sent him a text which read: 'Ha, ha but like I can't believe it – mad nite. XXXX.' Curran's response was to exhibit his awareness of the urgent need to distance himself from the awful crime just committed. 'F**k it. Delete message. Get a new number tomorrow,' he texted back to the young girl.

In fact, the series of mobile phone text messages between Curran, Keogh and the teenage girl in the hours after the double killing offered a grim, almost surreal insight into the mindset of those involved. There was little remorse, no trace of sympathy but ample evidence of a desire to do whatever was necessary not to be caught by the Gardaí or allow the double killing to be traced to Curran's door. The series of texts, outlined in court, read as follows:

Teen to Curran: 'Ha, I've just read what it says on the news. Ha, shittin.'

Curran to Teen: 'Ha, ha – you're mad.'

Teen to Curran: Ha, ha – but like I can't believe it. Mad nite XXX.'

Curran to Teen: 'F**k it. Delete message. Get a new number tomorrow.'

Teen to Curran: 'Why?'

Curran to Teen: 'If they ask ya for ur phone number XX.'

Keogh to Teen: 'Ring me XX.'

Curran to Teen: 'Ha.'

Teen to Curran: 'It's not funny shithead.'

Curran to Teen: 'Ah f**k it.'

Keogh to Teen: 'No problem. The man meant to be dead.'

Teen to Curran: 'Ah Schillachi, being all moany. I saved ur life.'

Curran to Teen: 'Ah ya, I luv ya.'

Keogh to Teen: 'Tell David Curran to ring me quick.'

Teen to Keogh: 'He's no credit. What's wrong.'

Teen to Curran: 'Sean said to ring quick.'

Curran to Teen: 'Can't.'

Keogh to Teen: 'Ask him to try someone else's phone.'

Teen to Curran: 'Ha, ha. I just texted him. Said no credit.'

Teen to Keogh: 'No what's wrong, no credit.'

Keogh to Teen: 'On Teletext about the other thing. We're f**cked.'

Teen to Keogh: 'I know, yeah.'

Keogh to Teen: 'I had to help my mate. I burnt my new runners and all.'

Teen to Keogh: 'No way XXX.'

Keogh to Teen: 'Swear to God, we're f**ked.'

Curran to Teen: 'Did u hear about that in Drimnagh. It's going around I done it cos I got stabbed other nite.'

Teen to Curran: 'No way.'

Curran to Teen: 'Yeah, f**kin weirdos. I wasn't in

Drimnagh all day.'

Teen to Curran: 'Yeah, I know ha ha. I have a plan but not going to text it.'

For the Kalite and Szwajkos families it was a brutal nightmare from which there was simply no escape. The victims' Irish employer, Alan Kennedy, was appalled at the manner in which the two mechanics had died and described them as model employees, skilled at their work and utterly devoted to their families back in Poland. Outside the court, Mr Kennedy effectively spoke for members of the two families who were overcome by grief when he explained he could see the despair unmistakably written in the eyes of the men's parents.

Throughout the trial, David Curran had insisted he had acted without intent on the evening of the double killing – maintaining that he was uncontrollable due to a cocktail of drink and drugs. One of the scariest elements of the case was how it lifted the lid on the lifestyle that some Irish teens now profess to live. His outline of his activities that 23 February day reads like an indictment of youth in modern Ireland. 'I went out about 10 a.m. that morning to the off licence. I bought a bottle of vodka and a few cans – and I went down to the canal, to the locks.' Curran fell into the company of three other young men and two teenage girls. One of the youths was Sean Keogh.

'We were drinking the vodka, smoking hash and swimming,' he told the court. 'We [also] had a few tablets – Roche D5s.' David Curran – who had left school at fifteen – had developed a serious addiction to Benzodiazepines, drugs nicknamed locally as 'Blueys' and 'Yellows'. He had been making efforts to kick his use of the drugs and had even had a scheduled meeting with an addiction counsellor just twenty-four hours before the fatal Benbulbin Road incident. But he had not cut back on his use of alcohol and cannabis. Eventually, the group tired of the canal and moved on to fields around St Michael's Estate in Inchicore where Curran found a heavy screwdriver. The group consumed a further two bottles of wine while Curran decided to hold on to the screwdriver as it might be useful for breaking into factories. Sometime along the way, a bag of alcopop drinks was also produced. Then the phone call from the teenager girl outside the chipper changed the course of the entire evening. Curran received three further phone calls as he made his way in mounting fury to Benbulbin Road.

'I was angry – I just ran to the chipper. Yeah, I was basically out of my head on it [drink and drugs]. I was stoned.' Curran insisted that when he arrived on Benbulbin Road he was lost to the cocktail of drink and drugs. 'I was roaring: "Who stabbed me Dad?" I ran up the road because there were people screaming that they were up there. There was a man and woman at a gate and another man at a porch door in the same garden. I was directed that it was them. I was screaming: "Was it yous?" The bald man was screaming back in his own language. The girl was trying to push him back from coming towards me so I went towards him and stabbed him.' Mariusz then came to his fallen friend's aid. 'He jumped over the railings. It made me go mad. So I stabbed him too as he was coming over the railings.'

For Eugene Szwajkos, nothing the Irish courts could do now to David Curran would ever replace his beloved son.

Mariusz had been the pride and joy of Eugene and his wife, Jamina, and had been utterly devoted to his family. He had liked working in Ireland – but insisted on ringing home regularly so as to keep in touch with all family developments in Poland. As with his friend Pawel, he spoke incessantly of one day being able to return permanently to Poland and build a prosperous, happy life there. Ireland may have been his opportunity but Poland was ultimately his home.

'Mariusz planned to stay in Ireland only until the summer – he was working in the Netherlands before so this was not his first time away,' Eugene explained. 'He missed Poland and he wanted to come back home. He loved his home.

'I talked to him on Skype [the free Internet phone service] just half an hour before he was attacked. I still cannot believe it. He said he was looking forward to coming home and to his sister's wedding in the summer.' The pain of discussing the horrific manner of his son's death remains difficult for Mr Szwajkos. In one interview with the *Irish Independent* after the sentencing hearing, he broke down sobbing, emotionally unable to continue. His only words were that the man who so brutally killed his son 'should burn' for his actions.

The heartbreaking images of the Szwajkos family escorting Mariusz's coffin to his Requiem Mass at the Church of Mary Magdalene in his small home town of Szczucin dominated the Irish papers in March 2008 – as did the poignant Polish tradition of covering the coffin with white flowers to represent lost youth and purity. Mariusz's siblings, Gosia, Rafal and Pawel, did their best to support their devastated parents – while Pawel Kalite's parents, Dariusz and Lucyna, were there to offer their own support.

Szczucin priest Fr Zygmunt Warchecha, pointed out that Mariusz made the ultimate sacrifice in going to the aid of his friend, Pawel, that awful day in Drimnagh. 'No love is greater than the sacrifice of giving your life up for your friends. [But] nobody has the right to take away anyone's life – [yet] you should not add evil to evil or death to death. You should not respond to death with rage.' Aptly, the Polish cleric warned that this was not a crime that impacted on only two families. He said: 'The death of Mariusz is a tragedy not only for his family and Poland but for Ireland.'

Yet, despite their pain, the family understood that the Irish nation could not be held responsible for the violent actions of one drug-fuelled teen. Mariusz' younger sister, Gosia, stressed after the trial that the family were deeply grateful for the kindness shown to them by Irish people – and that they did not hold the Irish people responsible for what had happened. It certainly helped that Gosia had herself spent time living and working in the west of Ireland – and had returned home with lots of happy memories. One of Mariusz's favourite photos was a snap of himself taken against the dramatic backdrop of the Cliffs of Moher in County Clare.

'My family and I want to thank the people of Ireland, particularly the hospital workers and the police who helped Mariusz before he died. My family does not wish to blame the people of Ireland and would prefer to think that this attack could have happened anywhere in the world. Mariusz was a very good, quiet man and part of my heart and my mother and father's hearts have died. The people who did this are not human,' said Gosia. The only comfort, she added, was that Mariusz had died trying to go to the aid of his friend and his family was deeply proud of that fact.

The pain was equally hard to cope with for the Kalite family. Pawel's grandmother, Celina, said the family would never recover from the sheer brutality and utter senselessness of the killings. 'We had a phone call from Pawel's aunt in Krakow who had heard from Pawel's room-mate in Dublin. As soon as we heard, Pawel's father drove to Krakow to catch a plane to Dublin,' she explained.

'We have received many letters from complete strangers in Ireland expressing their condolences and their sympathies. The Irish people have been wonderful as have Poles in Ireland living near to where Pawel lived.' Celina said that, given the brutal nature of the killings, Curran should now spend 'many, many years in prison'.

Just two hours before the fatal confrontation, Pawel had rung his aunt in Poland to schedule a trip home. His plan was to inquire into securing a mortgage so he could get an apartment for himself and his girlfriend. Pawel – like Mariusz – dreamed of going home and believed he had found the woman he wanted to spend the rest of his life with. It was a simple dream for a man who, when a small child, had suffered from repeated bouts of illness and ill health. But the Kalite family stressed that Pawel was always smiling – and he had grown up to be generous to a fault, always concerned about his family and friends. 'A stranger blew [out] the candle of life and cut the path of [his] life. He killed a good man and he destroyed the lives of his parents, sister and family,' the Kalite family said.

The Kalite and Szwajkos families also derived comfort from the fact that the killings were greeted with such a wave of horror and revulsion in Ireland and that so many ordinary people felt moved to express their solidarity with the families. As well as receiving hundreds of letters from ordinary Irish people – many from residents of Drimnagh – the families were touched that the then Taoiseach Bertie Ahern issued a personal message of condolence and expressed his disgust at what had happened on Benbulbin Road.

In Drimnagh, locals were determined to demonstrate that such violence was not part of their community and mounted a vigil outside the house where Pawel and Marius died. Drimnagh residents were soon joined by members of Ireland's Polish community, some of whom drove from Cork and Limerick to support their grieving compatriots. Business premises along Benbulbin Road also set up collections for the murder victims' parents. Some shops even displayed red-and-white Polish flags as a simple gesture of solidarity.

The Polish Embassy was quick to point out that, over the course of the Celtic Tiger era, Polish emigration to Ireland has been, by and large, a happy, rewarding and uniting experience for both cultures. The Polish Ambassador, Dr Tadeusz Szumowski, having ensured consular staff assisted the Kalite and Szwajkos families with the repatriation of the remains, pointed out that violence was not restricted to any single country – but had plagued virtually every corner of the modern world.

'It is really very tragic. We are all very sad but it is just, in a way, hooliganism, which has no borders, no frontiers. It could happen anywhere,' he said. Dr Szumowski also said that the families and the Polish people were very grateful for the sentiments expressed by Mr Ahern on behalf of the Irish people.

David Curran is serving two life sentences and his release date will be determined by the Parole Board. Their decision will be based on a number of factors including details of the trial transcript, Curran's behaviour while serving his prison sentence, his likely rehabilitation back into society and his age at the time of the offence. However, his release is unlikely to occur before 2024, at which stage he will be thirty-three years old.

Sean Keogh was sentenced to four years and six months in prison for his assault on Pawel Kalite. The final six months of the sentence were suspended. The prison term was handed down by Mr Justice McKechnie on 19 May 2010, less than two weeks after David Curran received his twin life sentences. It emerged that Keogh had a total of seventy-five convictions prior to his kicking the dying Pole in the head as he fell to the ground. His previous convictions included offences such as stealing cars, public order, Road Traffic Act breaches and criminal damage.

Mr Justice McKechnie warned that Keogh's criminal record was absolutely appalling and that he had delivered a vicious kick to dying man who was completely defenceless at the time. The judge said this action was to satisfy Keogh's lust for harm – and that the assault revealed a deep and sickening side to his personality. Mr Justice McKechnie added that Irish society had an entitlement not to be exposed to behaviour which he described as 'pure thuggery'.

Outside the court, the Keogh family issued an apology to the Kalite and Szwajkos families for what had happened. They also expressed their 'deep and heartfelt sorrow' to them on their loss.

Despite a Garda desire to bring public order charges against the two teenage girls and the fifteen-year-old boy who so dramatically inflamed the events on Benbulbin Road, the DPP, after considering a mammoth case file, which included 226 separate statements, ruled against such a move. The two teenage girls and the fifteen-year-old boy were instead dealt with under the juvenile liaison scheme. They will have no convictions recorded against them and their identities were protected throughout the entire court proceedings because of their age.

10

Donal Manley

'He was an easy target'

For a quiet, shy man, Donal Manley (sixty-two) had a lot of friends. Maybe it was due to his having worked in bars across Cork city throughout his life. Maybe it was down to his love of the arts scene, which made him a familiar face at theatres, cinemas and exhibitions. Perhaps it was his love of a good conversation over a pint. Yet the greatest explanation is probably the fact that Donal was, in Irish parlance, 'a true gent'.

Donal was best known for his easy smile, his relaxed manner and his kindness. Not surprisingly, they were traits that endeared him to anyone who crossed his path whether it was via his work or his social life. Neighbours found Donal a joy to live near – he was considerate to his elderly neighbours, no favour was too great to ask him and he took pride in the High Street community, just off Cork's city centre, that he called home.

In fact, Donal's house was like a show-home – it was always kept immaculately and, while he was originally from the countryside, some seven miles outside Cork city, he loved the fact that High Street was just a short stroll from all the major city centre attractions, be it the cinema, Opera House, Everyman Palace Theatre or various arts venues.

In fact, Donal was such a familiar face around the area that people quickly noticed his absence in October 2008. He had not been seen walking to get milk or the newspaper at his local shop. Neighbours noted that that was unusual because Donal was such a creature of habit and you could almost set your watch by his morning routine.

The last sighting locally of Donal came on 10 October when a neighbour, Barry Kelly, saw him on the street and stopped to exchange a few words. The last time he saw Donal Manley was when the retired barman was standing talking to two men near a van parked on the street.

By 12 October, when there still had been no sign of Donal, his friends and neighbours began to worry. What concerned them most was that the lights had been switched on in Donal's house throughout the entire weekend and his curtains had not been drawn. Eventually, neighbours became concerned enough to check the house. Neighbours Donal and Cathy Kelly peered through the window for any sign of Donal and were alarmed by what they saw. There were clear signs of a disturbance when they looked through the window of the house that Sunday evening at 7.30 p.m. The furniture was askew and it appeared that a table had been overturned. They also spotted what appeared to be a pair of upright shoes behind a couch.

It was sufficient to alarm them both and the Gardaí were immediately alerted. Officers decided to check on the retiree at his home at 68 High Street to ensure that everything was well. When Garda Jim Smiddy finally managed to get into the house, the true horror of Donal's fate finally became known. The 62-year-old's body was discovered, lying on the floor near the couch, with his face and chest covered in dried blood.

Within a fortnight, Gardaí were following a definite line of inquiry. Bizarrely, they had received numerous eyewitness reports of a man spotted walking from the High Street area that October weekend carrying an umbrella and a flat-screen TV. Detectives examined CCTV security camera footage from the area and from the premises where Donal Manley was known to have been socialising in the 24-hour period before his death.

Patricia O'Leary, owner of the Cork Arms Bar on MacCurtain Street, told Gardaí that Donal Manley was a local in the pub and was there on the night of 9 October 2009. She had chatted with him and he said that if he didn't see her sooner he would see her around the jazz weekend in two weeks' time. He appeared to be in very good form. Another man, Michael O'Connor, who works as part of the security staff at the Old Oak Bar on Oliver Plunkett Street, stated that shortly before 1 a.m. on 10 October, Mr Manley arrived and appeared to have had a few drinks as his speech was slightly slurred. However, he was polite, chatty and was admitted to the bar.

Having reviewed the CCTV footage, Gardaí quickly decided they wanted to speak to Paul Murphy (twenty-five) of 57 Kilmore Road, Knocknaheeny, Cork, in relation to the events on High Street.

The manner of Donal's death was truly horrific. Murphy's subsequent Central Criminal Court trial in Cork heard Assistant State Pathologist Dr Declan Gilsenan describe how Donal Manley's injuries were consistent with a violent assault. 'The injuries to the side of the head and jaw [indicate] side-to-side compression; the mostly likely cause of these would be some kind of standing on the head, probably on the right side when the left side was in contact with the floor,' Dr Gilsenan testified. Findings of fractures to the thyroid cartilage were explained as being consistent with manual strangulation of a person being held in a neck-lock or someone standing on the head, he added. The post mortem examination confirmed that Donal had his jaw broken in two different places, he had two fractures to the left cheekbone, one to the right cheekbone, extensive fracture at the base of the skull and fractures of the thyroid cartilage, bruising around the face especially around the eyes.

'The cause of death was bruising of the brain and intracranial haemorrhage secondary to, or associated with, fracture of the skull. The injuries are typical of a bad fight . . . that type of thing with some kicking of the head. The degree of injuries otherwise is really only seen in a bad road accident or where a jacked-up car falls down on someone. It requires considerable force to the side of the head,' Dr Gilsenan added.

When the pathologist examined the body at the scene following the grim discovery by Gardaí, it was lying behind a sofa curled up into a foetal position, as if for protection. The head and neck were soaked in blood. Parts of the house were also blood-spattered.

That October weekend, Paul Murphy arrived at his then-girlfriend's home in a dishevelled and confused condition. Michelle Wall had been watching the *X-Factor* TV show with her friend Lorraine Pearse, when Murphy suddenly arrived carrying a flat-screen TV. Both women were concerned about his demeanour.

Ms Pearse told the Central Criminal Court that Murphy had explained to them that he had been drinking in a man's house and had hit him once. Asked if Murphy had explained why he had hit the man, Ms Pearse said: 'He said the man tried to put his hand down his pants. Paul said he wasn't like that, he tried it again and Paul lost it, he said.'

Ms Pearse explained that Murphy was drunk and was acting very bizarrely at the time. Defence counsel, Blaise O'Carroll SC, in cross-examination, brought the witness through a statement she made to Gardaí and she did not contest any details.

'He [Paul] stormed into his bedroom. Michelle went in after him. I heard him saying to Michelle he wanted to leave and hand himself into the guards, he should have gone before. There was an argument going on between Paul and Michelle. She kept telling him to calm down and get some sleep as he was out of it.'

'[Later Paul said] he met this man, he couldn't remember

where. The man invited him back to his house. He had a few drinks with the man. Paul said yer man put his hand down his private parts. Paul said he was not into that. The man said OK but Paul said the man done it again. He said he lost it and gave him a punch in the head. The man was on the floor, he took the telly and the box. He could hear a gurgling sound from the man's throat on the ground. [Paul said] "I don't know if he is dead or alive",' she said.

Murphy was arrested by Gardaí a few days after the murder and brought to the Bridewell Garda Station for questioning. In one interview with Detective Sergeant Shane Bergin, which was later read out to the murder trial, Murphy said he deeply regretted his actions. 'I am so sorry, I apologise so much for killing him.' Murphy told Gardaí he did not remember how he ended up in the house but that he had passed out after drinking rum and awoke to find a man trying to put his hand down his pants.

He said he punched him twice and that as he left he thought: 'F**k this pr**k, after what he done to me I stole his television.' But Murphy insisted to Gardaí that he had not intended to seriously harm the elderly man.

Murphy then told Gardaí the next morning that he was not happy with his earlier reply and he wanted to clarify what he had said: 'I didn't actually know I actually killed him or not. I am sincerely sorry for all I done and I am sorry to his family as well – I didn't intend on hurting that person at all.' Murphy insisted to Gardaí he couldn't even recall what the man [Donal Manley] even looked like.

Murphy told Gardaí he recalled telling friends that he had robbed a house and hit a man but he did not think he had killed him. He later heard reports on Cork local radio stations 96FM and RedFM of a man being killed in a house but did not think that was where he had been. It was only when Gardaí had called to his mother's house and he heard about the call that he realised the full significance of those radio reports.

'I got a bag of cocaine and tried to drown my sorrows, [try to] take the pain away,' Murphy said. He told Gardaí that, in the week before the incident, he had been taking prescription tablets including Diazepam and Rohypnol. He had also been drinking very heavily.

Gardaí again asked Murphy to recall the circumstances surrounding the incident in which Donal Manley was struck. Murphy explained that: 'When I woke up he was trying to put his hand down my pants. I threw his hand away. I was still fairly out of it, I tried to go back to sleep. [But] the person tried it again. Then the man stood up, I stood up too [from the couch]. I said, "What the f**k do you think you're doing?" And I gave him a dig. When he swung back I gave him another dig.'

Murphy insisted to Gardaí that there was another man in the house at the time. This man, he claimed, woke up due to the sound of the row and demanded to know what was going on. He then fell back to sleep. In later interviews, Murphy identified this man. However, when Gardaí checked with the man, he had a verifiable alibi that placed him elsewhere at the time. When this was put to Murphy, he replied: 'Sure anyone could provide an alibi.'

Gardaí also pointed out that the man, when confronted by detectives with what Murphy had claimed, said he had not spoken to the defendant for a period of at least a year following a row. The man was adamant he was not in the High Street flat that evening with Murphy. In contrast, Murphy was adamant that he had settled his differences with the man three weeks before Donal Manley's death.

Murphy told Gardaí that after leaving Donal Manley's house he went to a flat at Dominic Street where his girlfriend lived. But he insisted that he did not bring the television to that flat. 'I put it in a black bag and hid it in Shandon graveyard. I then got rid of it when I realised it was broken.'

The meticulous Garda investigation had also revealed crucial clues about the horrific events that occurred in Donal Manley's home. A palm print matching Murphy's was found on a door frame in the blood of the deceased, indicating that blood was on his hand. When questioned by Gardaí, Murphy replied: 'I don't remember having blood on my hands but I am not denying it.'

Gardaí had also determined that Murphy met up with Donal Manley close to the Morrison's Island footbridge, not far from Cork College of Commerce, off the city centre. Murphy admitted that, at the time, he was armed with a screwdriver concealed in his pocket. He explained to Gardaí that his original intention was to steal from cars that evening.

A detective asked Murphy if it was his intention to go back and rob the man [Donal Manley]. Murphy replied: 'It was an opportunity to see if I could get extra money – [but] I wasn't going to hurt him.'

Murphy insisted to Gardaí he had only thrown two punches, but Gardaí put it to him that the injuries sustained by Donal Manley indicated a far more severe attack. 'The injuries are more consistent with a frenzied attack, someone losing their cool and hitting the deceased multiple times,' a Garda said. Murphy replied: 'I don't remember if I kept hitting the man or not. It is possible [I lost it] but I am not sure.'

Murphy also insisted that an injury to his hand was sustained several days later when he punched a wall in the city centre after getting very upset. He was adamant it had not happened in Donal Manley's High Street home. He said he could not recall standing on Donal Manley's head or attempting to strangle him. 'Jesus, I don't remember anything like that. I wasn't thinking straight, I wasn't in my right frame of mind . . . I was really, really stoned.'

However, State prosecutor, Mary Ellen Ring SC, later pointed out to the trial that Murphy made sixteen phone calls over a four-hour period that day, involving a total of five different people. '[It] shows someone who was very much in it rather than out of it,' she argued.

Mr Justice Paul Carney, after concluding arguments from the State and the defence legal team, placed the jury in charge. The jury of nine women and three men took just two hours and twenty-four minutes to reach their unanimous decision that Paul Murphy had, in fact, murdered Donal Manley. The conviction carried a mandatory life sentence. Murphy was also convicted of having stolen Donal Manley's property. When he was jailed for life, Murphy gave no outward, visible reaction. He briefly acknowledged a few relatives in court before being led away by Prison Service officers to commence his life term.

That afternoon, just one week after St Patrick's Day, the

Manley family assembled at Cork Courthouse on Washington Street. In ways, it was their final gesture to Donal – a final chance to explain just what a kind yet vulnerable man their brother was. Most of all it was a chance to try to defend his good name. The previous weeks had been a truly traumatic experience for the family.

Such a trial would have been ordeal enough even without the claims that Murphy had made about Donal Manley. The claims had deeply shocked, appalled and outraged the family. Murphy's murder conviction and the mandatory life sentence he received were cold comfort for the manner in which the family felt Donal's name had been dragged through the mud.

The case had left the Manley family reeling. The manner of Donal's death was shocking enough. The quiet, reserved barman had suffered horrific head injuries – and the realisation that one injury was consistent with someone having stamped on his skull was shocking in the extreme. Murphy's decision to then steal items belonging to Donal was explained as the result of his extreme intoxication at the time. The items were valued at just over €600.

In the minutes before Paul Murphy was handed a mandatory life sentence, the Manley family got their final opportunity, via a victim impact statement, to explain how the horrific crime had impacted upon them. They also got a chance to defend their sibling. Donal's brother, Pat, said that his brother had not only been physically attacked but his character and good name had also been assaulted.

'Donal had in recent years retired from the bar trade as a result of arthritis in his legs, which made it difficult for him to stand for long periods of time,' Pat told the court. 'Already small in stature, this condition further diminished his size and he walked with a distinctive amble. I cannot help but to think that he presented an easy target for those who seek out the weak and the vulnerable to prey on to fuel their non-productive lives.'

Mr Manley said his family were appalled at the manner in which his brother's character was attacked during the trial. 'Particularly painful was to hear details of the violent nature of Donal's death and the vicious and slanderous statements made against his character during the course of the trial. Such statements are easily made when the person is no longer around to defend themselves.'

Donal's sister, Mary Greene, said they were absolutely devastated by the precise details of how their brother was killed. 'Donal could not defend himself and he was killed by this man. It was a cowardly, unprovoked and brutal attack in his own home. This has been very difficult for all the family. Donal was such a happy-go-lucky, decent, kind man.'

To onlookers it was clear that the claims levelled during the trial process had been almost as upsetting to the family as the graphic details of the fatal injuries Donal had sustained. The Manleys felt that Donal had not only been killed but his good name had been assassinated as well.

Paul Murphy was as different from Donal Manley as chalk is from cheese. Murphy was twenty-four at the time of the killing – and a strong, powerfully built young man compared to the slight, arthritic, elderly figure of Donal Manley. Donal had never come to Garda attention in any manner, but Paul Murphy had, in his brief twenty-four years, already earned twenty-three previous convictions. Three of these were for assault causing harm – one of which involved striking a person with a glass and then attempting to stamp on their head.

Paul Murphy now faces getting out of prison when he will be close to his fortieth year. But, for the extended Manley family, there is no release from the painful memories of the shocking and brutal death that the inoffensive barman met in the sanctuary of his own home.

11

Society

Violence, sadly, is nothing new or unique to Irish society. Neither, for that matter, is substance abuse, with alcohol having played a destructive role in Irish history for centuries. In fact, the connection between alcohol and violence has long been known within Irish culture and the stereotypical image of the drunken Irishman is, tragically, all too common throughout the world. Instances of the influence of alcohol on Irish society – and major events in Irish history – are sadly plentiful.

The Battle of Kinsale in 1601, for example, saw beer being given to Irish soldiers to fortify them for the horrors of the coming battle – with one drunken soldier later apparently providing key details of what the Gaelic chieftains intended when captured by the British commander. The Siege of Derry in 1689 was broken when, according to Loyalist accounts, a boom across the harbour was successfully breached by armed merchant ships because Irish Jacobite soldiers manning the cannons on shore were so drunk their aim was next to useless.

In his famous book, *The Gangs of New York*, author Herbert Asbury paints a depressing picture of the link between poor, illiterate Irish immigrants and alcohol abuse at the 'Five Points', New York's notorious nineteenth-century slum. The immigrants may have brought poverty with them – but they also brought a destructive taste for alcohol and a clearly related propensity for violent crime.

However, the question arises whether our modern, highly educated and more evolved society is a less safe place than the Ireland of thirty, fifty or seventy years ago? A key difference is that while Ireland always had examples of alcohol abuse throughout history, drugs are an entirely modern phenomenon – and a dangerous ingredient to the already potent cocktail of alcohol and violence.

The bulk of modern Irish homicides fall into two broad categories – gang-related and 'traditional' where the motives can vary from sexual, emotional (jealousy or anger), financial or psychotic. However, in both broad categories the so-called trigger factor for the fatal attack can often directly and indirectly be linked to substance abuse, be it alcohol or drugs. For instance, over the past decade, particularly in Dublin and Limerick, most gang-related homicides are connected with aspects of the drug trade ranging from turf wars to assassinations associated with unpaid drug debts. In the more traditional forms of homicide, the fatal attack can often be inextricably linked to bouts of drug or alcohol use. One US study showed that alcohol and drugs, in non-gang-related homicides, can prove a significant trigger-factor in six out of ten cases. But alcohol and drug abuse is an even bigger factor in non-fatal violent crime.

The heroin epidemic in inner city Dublin in the 1970s and 1980s demonstrated just how addiction could fuel a major crime wave. The legacy of Celtic Tiger affluence is now a nationwide scourge of addicts whose drugs tastes range from cocaine to heroin and from Ecstasy to amphetamines.

In just one day covering Cork Circuit Criminal Court last year I thought it was worth noting that of eighteen cases in the day's list, sixteen ultimately involved either drugs or alcohol abuse as a factor in some shape or form. In the District Court, the links are often far, far worse – particularly on a Monday morning when judges face the aftermath of a weekend's drinking in Ireland's towns and cities.

The problem for Ireland is that while current crime rates are far from the worst ever recorded on this island, the eras that delivered the worst rates on record all relate to periods of dramatic political and civil unrest. Today, violent crime rates are slowly but steadily increasing – fuelled by record levels of alcohol and drug abuse – despite the fact we live in an affluent, liberal democracy that has now been at peace for decades.

While alcohol abuse has been a perennial issue on Irish shores, modern consumption rates – largely thanks to economic factors and greater disposable incomes – are now dwarfing previous consumption figures. Combined with drugs, it has made for a lethal cocktail that has borne tragic consequences in blood on Irish streets and in Irish homes.

Alcohol Action Ireland (AAI) expressed shock in December 2009 when the government announced plans to cut excise rates on some alcohol products – warning that consumption rates were already a matter of serious concern. In August 2010, AAI director Fiona Ryan said that teens are now able to get intoxicated in Ireland for as little as €6.

'While we welcome the overall reduction in youth crime figures as well as the 22 per cent drop in alcohol offences in 2009, the fact remains that the largest category of youth offences are still alcohol-related. According to the Garda Diversion Programme's 2009 Annual Report, some 17.6 per cent of youth crimes were categorised as alcohol offences.

'However, we already know that alcohol is a factor in many other youth crimes, including, for instance, public order and criminal offences. We also know from the Irish Youth Justice Service that most young people gain access to alcohol with "relative ease". Added to that, the widespread availability of cheap alcohol means that children and young people can get drunk on pocket-money prices, with cans of beer being sold for as little as 67 cent each and bottles of vodka retailing for less than €12. When we consider that the Office of Tobacco Control estimated that the average Irish sixteen- to seventeen-year-old was spending around €20 a week on alcohol, then €20 has the potential to buy a lot more alcohol that it used to,' she said.

The problem – as highlighted by numerous Irish addiction treatment centres – is that alcohol is now widely recognised as a 'gateway' substance to other drugs. The subsequent combination of both is often explosive. The greater the exposure to alcohol and the younger the age at which it happens, the greater the chances of that individual getting involved with harder drugs – and, tragically, in a minority of cases, violent crime.

In 2006, Ireland recorded its then highest-ever homicide rate recorded for a period of civil calm – with 66 people being killed, an increase of almost 7 per cent on the 2005 total. The same year saw incidents of assault causing harm spiral by 20 per cent and drug dealing rose by 13 per cent. As RTÉ's Crime Correspondent, Paul Reynolds, accurately noted, Ireland had not witnessed an explosion in violent crime – but rather a steady, gradual increase over the period of a decade.

'If you take the longer-term view, say over the past thirty years, the increase is far more evident. There were twenty-two homicides in 1976. That had risen to thirty-five by 1981. So I think you can say that violent crime has been increasing, steadily, not dramatically. It's really been a case of three steps up and one or two steps back depending on the year. However, since the 1970s more and more people have been dying violently and arguably this generation is more violent than the previous one,' he said.

'However, what is perhaps more disturbing is not the increase in the figures but the increase in the level of violence associated with these crimes. It's not the number but the type of crimes today that should shock people. In the 1950s, the country would have been convulsed by a case where a farmer shot another farmer in a row over land. It would have dominated the newspapers for weeks. Today such a crime would make the front page for one day. Today it takes something far more tragic, unusual or violent to garner widespread media attention,' he pointed out.

As we have seen, killings like those of Manuela Riedo, Pawel Kalite, Mariusz Szwajkos and Sophie Toscan du Plantier have had a huge impact on Irish society. This is as much down to the fact that they involved non-Irish nationals as to the appalling violence that featured in each and every case. Newspaper editorials over the period of each killing are instructive in that they again and again raise questions over the type of society that Ireland is evolving into.

Many have highlighted the fact that the violence at which Ireland often looks, wide-eyed on TV screens, blighting the streets of London, Manchester, Glasgow and even New York is now evident in Dublin, Limerick, Cork, Waterford and Galway.

Yet, to put Ireland properly in context, by international standards this is still not an overly violent country. Far from it. In fact, international statistics put Ireland to the lower end of the scale in terms of violent crime. In 2002, the eighth United Nations international crime trends study ranked Ireland thirty-second in terms of crimes committed per capita of population. Ireland was sandwiched at a crime rate of 20.23 per 1,000 people between Russia in thirty-first place and Bulgaria in thirty-third. The United States was ranked eighth, the UK sixth and South Africa tenth. Papua New Guinea and Yemen were at the bottom of the list with the lowest per capita crime rates.

But if homicide rates are considered in an international context, Ireland soars to a far better performance – with our homicide rate dwarfed by those of our Western neighbours. Ireland's latest homicide rate – which is the number of homicides committed per 100,000 of population – is 1.12.

We are only marginally worse than Switzerland (1.01) which has for years been considered one of the world's safest countries and held up as a model of successful modern society. Compared to Ireland, countries like Brazil (25.2), South Africa (37), Russia (14.9) and Jamaica (59) seem lethal by comparison with homicide rates that are virtually off the chart.

But the fact is that, taken over a fifty-year period, Ireland's violent crime statistics are getting much worse. In a special 2010 report, the World Health Organisation (WHO) ranked Ireland worst in Europe for violent knife crime. The grim fact remains that Ireland is not as safe as it once was. In the space of just thirty years, Ireland's homicide rate has more than tripled – and it is no coincidence that the same period is generally defined as the rolling out of Ireland's drug abuse problem.

A further issue, somewhat ironically, was the resolution of the Northern Ireland conflict following a painstaking and often tortuous peace process. The ending of paramilitary violence was a boon to the long-suffering Northern Ireland community – and, indeed, their neighbours in the Republic and UK. However, peace did not meet with widespread approval with many former paramilitaries drifting into the criminal world of drugs, extortion or smuggling.

Worse still, other paramilitaries became 'guns for hire' to major criminal gangs and also brought with them a lethal knowledge of how to obtain military-type weaponry. Limerick is a stark example in point. Gun crime in Limerick in the 1970s and early 1980s was largely unheard of and what occurred usually involved shotguns or old revolvers.

But, since 2000, Limerick's gangs have attempted – and often succeeded – in getting their hands on weaponry more suited to a modern European army.

In April 2007, Cork Circuit Criminal Court heard that British agents from the Special Organised Crime Agency, working with Gardaí, had foiled a plot by one notorious Limerick gang to source weapons from an individual they thought was an East European arms dealer. The deal – incredibly negotiated, in part, through an Irish prison – involved the gang demanding Kalashnikov AKM assault rifles, RPG-7 rocket-launchers, Uzi sub-machine guns (of the same type that arm the Gardaí) as well as a host of powerful semi-automatic pistols.

The gang made absolutely no secret to the undercover UK police officers what the weapons were intended for: they planned to conduct a series of targeted assassinations and wipe out their rivals. Such was the sophistication involved in the arms-smuggling attempt – and the brutal intent of the gang – trial Judge Patrick Moran admitted to being appalled by the possible consequences for Ireland if the attempt had succeeded.

It is a point worth noting that the Limerick arms-smuggling attempt was entirely linked to a feud between gangs over control of the city's money-spinning drug supply network. Drugs had delivered profits so great to the Limerick – and Dublin – gangs that they could easily afford to try to equip themselves as small private armies.

It is a similar story with drug smuggling. Gangs now have access to so much money that their resources often dwarf those of the agencies trying to foil them, including the

Naval Service, Customs & Excise, Gardaí and Air Corps. In July 2007, Ireland savoured its biggest-ever offshore cocaine seizure with €440 million worth of Columbian drugs seized in Dunlough Bay in west Cork. Pointedly, the seizure only occurred because one of the gang members filled an outboard engine with diesel instead of petrol – and the craft overturned in heavy seas after the engine subsequently failed.

The trial of the men responsible underlined just how much European gangs invest in defeating State authorities and getting drug shipments to market. The Circuit Criminal Court heard that Garda movements are monitored in the run-up to a shipment's arrival, sophisticated, encrypted communications gear is used and fleets of high-powered cars and boats are provided to swiftly ferry the drugs to market. In contrast, some State agencies are expected to foil such shipments while operating on a shoestring budget. The Customs & Excise service, for instance, has two dedicated cutters to patrol Ireland's entire coastline. The Naval Service had been planning to replace three ships which are at the end of their recommended service lives. All are now expected to remain in service for years longer than anticipated.

It is little wonder that drug prices have plummeted as supplies pour into Ireland and Europe from Asia and South America. In the space of just three years, the street price of cocaine in Ireland fell by more than 35 per cent – a price decline entirely attributed to oversupply.

So great has alcohol and substance abuse become that doctors now blame it as a factor in 80 per cent of all admissions to Accident and Emergency (A&E) units nationwide after 11 p.m. One of Ireland's most experienced emergency medicine consultants is Dr Chris Luke. He has worked at some of the busiest hospitals in Cork and major UK cities – and he argues that spiral of violence now being experienced is directly proportionate to the high consumption of alcohol and drugs.

In an article for the *Evening Echo* in May 2010, Dr Luke warned that the greatest single threat now facing young people on modern Ireland is drug-related violence. 'It comes as no surprise to those contending with the present plague of drug misuse. Indeed, [some] cases offer a textbook example of "limbic" violence – that drug-fuelled derangement of the limbic system – the appetite and impulse-controlling network within the brain – which is so commonly responsible for atrocities of war as well as so many recent murders in this country,' he wrote.

'Increasingly frequently, hospital staffs have to deal with maniacal, young drug-takers with temporary but super-human strength. Last month, for instance, it yet again took numerous burly adults, handcuffs and huge quantities of medical sedatives to contain a slender but strong adolescent female in one of our emergency departments in Cork (courtesy of a head-shop high).

'The specific agents matter less than the fact that drug-taking leads inevitably to extraordinary and terrifying levels of violence. The scientific basis of this involves the so-called "paradoxical excitation". In other words, intoxicants like alcohol, cannabis and sleeping tablets – which we are told were consumed by the killer of the two Polish men [Mariusz Szwajkos and Pawel Kalite] – can have the opposite effect to the usual relaxation-sedation expected and can provoke extreme agitation and violence in a small but significant proportion of users.

'Given the upward trajectory of violent crime in this country, so closely mirroring our appetite for drugs of all sorts and, given the continuing denial by so many apologists for cannabis and legal highs etc that their favourite chemicals have any role in violence (or indeed almost any medical mishap), it is becoming vital that basic drug screening such as urine testing be undertaken as part of the early investigation of all serious violent crime.

'A beneficial side-effect would be a potential reduction in the number of unexpected deaths in police custody as the use of such drugs as methadone and cocaine can be fatal but it is often not apparent during the arrest of violent adults.

'Such epidemiological investigation in France has revealed that about 9 per cent of road fatalities are associated with the consumption of cannabis, for instance. Now, arguably, the greatest single threat to the safety and welfare of young people in this country is drug-related violence (including impulsive suicide). The apologists will reach for their usual "but alcohol causes far more problems than drugs" hypothesis but this must be significantly rebutted. Drink and drugs are – like malaria and measles – distinctive but equally deadly in their effects.

'And a combination of the two is infinitely more dangerous than the constituent parts as exemplified in the tale of the young man who admitted to being out of control before launching his terrifying and terrible attack on Mr Szwajkos and Mr Kalite. If one good result could emerge from this sad story it would be a clear picture of the correlation between drug and alcohol consumption and violence.

'Again, the apologists may add that correlation is not

causation. But it is a very good start – like the all too evident remorse of the young killer in this case. Once fully sober, [it] would at least show clearly that cannabis, cocaine, mephedrone or synthetic cannibols do not stop people becoming extremely violent. In due course, as was eventually realized with alcohol, the causative relationship between drug taking of any sort and hideous violence will become obvious – even to the most wishful of thinkers. Truly, at this stage, other educational efforts would seem to be relatively frivolous and [an] expensive waste of time – and lives.'

The Dublin-based Merchants Quay Project – which has worked for years to help drug addicts – estimated in one 2004 report that there were 15,000 heroin users in Ireland. The Health Research Board (HRB) acknowledged in 2006 that drug use – particularly of 'hard drugs' including cocaine and heroin – had now firmly become a national rather than a Dublin-based problem. Between 2001 and 2006 a total of 68,754 people were treated for drug abuse problems and they ranged in age from fifteen to sixty-four years.

Interestingly, in 2006 the breakdown of problem drugs was cannabis (41 per cent), opiates (39 per cent) and cocaine (9 per cent). However, in the space of three years, the cocaine problem is estimated to have substantially increased – with one Circuit Criminal Court trial being told that cocaine was now so readily available and had been so reduced in price that it had driven down the price of Ecstasy by almost 80 per cent.

The geographic trends in drug abuse in Ireland also makes for stark reading. HRB director of alcohol and drug research Dr Jean Long warned in 2006 that some parts of Ireland had recorded astonishing increases in drug use. 'The relatively small increase in new cases nationally masks stark trends in Health Service Executive (HSE) areas over the six-year period. For example; the number of new cases increased by 100 per cent in the Western area, which includes Galway, Mayo and Roscommon.'

Between 2001 and 2006 the numbers of drug cases in other areas soared by: 76 per cent South East (Carlow, Kilkenny, Waterford, Wexford and Tipperary South); 57 per cent Midlands (Offaly, Laois, Longford and Westmeath); 37 per cent North East (Cavan, Louth, Meath and Monaghan) and 33 per cent Mid-West (Clare, Limerick and Tipperary North).

The problem is that just as Ireland was late to wake up to the threat posed by drugs in the 1970s, the country seems slow to catch on to the need to properly fund tackling addiction through the support bodies that have evolved. In 2010, Ireland's prison population spiralled over the 5,000 mark for the first time in modern history – yet Ireland closed Spike Island prison in 2004 as a cost-saving measure despite the fact it had amongst the best educational and rehabilitation facilities of any Irish prison.

In July 2010 the 75th World Convention of Alcoholics Anonymous was staged in San Antonio, Texas. One of the most common catchphrases at the convention was: 'I am sober today thanks to the grace of God and the judge.' It is a similar story for Narcotics Anonymous in the US. That is because ongoing attendance at such self-help support groups is now recognised by the US judiciary as central to tackling the problem that often lurks at the heart of the crime – namely the addiction itself.

The Rutland Centre estimates that one in ten Irish people now drink alcoholically – and while the majority will never get involved in serious or violent crime, a significant number inevitably will. Crucially, it is likely that these individuals would never darken the doorway of a court or Garda station but for their addiction. Of even greater concern is Ireland's spiralling rate of underage drinking. The Matt Talbot Adolescent Services revealed in a study that 70 per cent of youngsters have been abusing some form of substance – alcohol, drugs or aerosol solvents – since the age of eleven. By June 2010, the centre had received 212 referrals at their Cork centre for young men aged under eighteen years – compared to 278 for all of 2009.

In the US, attendance at residential treatment programmes is routinely ordered for offenders by judges – and they go further by insisting that defendants show stamped attendance books from AA or NA meetings. The core point is that they believe addressing the root cause of the problem will ultimately avoid the criminality symptom. In contrast, while Irish judges and the Probation Service try to utilise treatment centres, it is on a haphazard basis with waiting lists for drug addiction treatment centres particularly long. Sometimes it can take months to secure a place on a course. Stamped attendance books for AA or NA meetings are unheard of – and such is the pressure now on Ireland's Probation Service that judges were warned in 2009 that they had to clearly prioritise cases requiring probation reports. Otherwise, it could take the Probation Service upwards of three months to get the report ready. In rare cases the delay can extend up to six months.

By late 2009, the Probation and Welfare Service (PWS) was operating with an estimated 20 per cent reduction in staffing levels compared to 2007 levels because of Ireland's fiscal crisis. The service was increasingly unable to complete probation reports, as requested by the courts, in the usual eight-week time frame.

The PWS – like all other elements of the public service – was subject to the government's recruitment ban with all new positions only being filled with the confirmation of the Department of Finance. The PWS was forced to write a letter to all judges explaining the reality of their resources and asked that priority be given to cases where individuals are deemed likely to pose a risk of reoffending. In what seemed a self-perpetuating nightmare to many, the very service that aimed to help tackle reoffending was being financially cut off at the knees.

The entire question of rehabilitation was highlighted four years earlier when Senator Ivana Bacik pointed out that one study indicated that rehabilitation within the community was twice as effective as prison-based rehab programmes. Unfortunately, community-based rehab for offenders is not as appealing at the polls as a 'get tough with crime' message.

Ireland got its own dose of this in 1997 with the 'zero tolerance' approach when Fianna Fáil came to power after a general election in which they promised a historic crackdown on crime, particularly violent assaults and drug-related offences. In the UK, Michael Howard pioneered the now-infamous 'prison works' policy which saw numbers in UK prisons soar over the next decade. In 1992, the UK had roughly 45,000 people behind bars – but by 2008 this had soared close to 70,000 inmates. It was a costly policy, requiring expensive new prisons not to mention the huge annual cost of keeping people behind bars. Unfortunately, it did not work in terms of slashing back on the overall crime rate though there were a few statistical successes.

Now faced with a fiscal and economic crisis, the UK is moving away from the 'prison works' philosophy with Lord Chancellor Ken Clarke indicating that rehabilitation may get more emphasis over the coming years. A key element in that will be offering aid to offenders with addiction problems on their release from custody. A significant proportion of those who reoffend after release from prison – some studies indicate as high as 80 per cent – do so as a direct result of addiction issues with alcohol and drugs.

The reoffending rate itself is a cause for huge concern. In the UK it has hovered around 60 per cent for the past decade – and Ireland's figure is estimated to be only slightly lower. Crucially, this means that of the adult criminal population, almost six out of ten can be expected to be convicted of a criminal offence within two years of being released. One Home Office study showed that of these re-convicted offenders, a staggering 89 per cent have problems in relation to alcohol and drugs.

The 'revolving door' prison is not just restricted to the UK – and any court reporter in Ireland will verify the fact. My own reporting experiences underline this – with my notes showing that the record reoffender I reported on came three years ago when a 34-year-old was said in the District Court to have more than 200 previous convictions. The man had both alcohol and drug problems.

The long-term prognosis for Irish society remains problematic. There appears to be a reluctance and increasingly an inability to fund proper, community-based rehab programmes for those for whom drugs and alcohol are clearly a factor in crime. In the case of violent offenders, addiction problems are routinely cited as a mitigating factor in sentencing, with little follow-up on the commitment to treatment.

The problem is further compounded by the manner in which violence is depicted within society. While the media offer saturation coverage on all major violent crimes and the woes of modern society, other media forms depict violence in a dramatically different fashion. A study by Yale-New Haven Teachers Institute found that violence is increasingly regarded by American teens as an acceptable manner in which to deal with specific problems: 'With school violence on the rise, experts say middle schools must provide alternatives to help children. If teens have nothing to do, they will find ways to get into trouble. Children need role models. They need to see the adults in their lives taking action against violence. [Yet] society today is full of evidence of violent behavior. Everywhere we look there is violence on television, in our home, school and community,' report author Carolyn Kinder explained.

Part of the issue for Ireland is that one of the most traditional influences on society – the Catholic Church – has been itself reeling from a succession of scandals. Since the first clerical child abuse controversies rocked the Church in the late 1980s, the influence of the Church on Irish society has waned to a significant degree – and, in the resultant vacuum, the social stigma that surrounded violent crime has inevitably weakened.

So great was the concern over the revelations about abuses both current and historic that Pope Benedict XVI issued a pastoral letter in early 2010 to attempt to address the matter. The irony was not lost on people that at the very time Irish society needed an influential moral compass, the Church was left battling to address and rectify the appalling neglect and abuse of some of the most vulnerable members of Irish society.

This leaves Ireland facing into an increasingly uncertain future. The picture is one of an increasingly addicted society lurching towards ever higher violent crime rates and a dramatically restricted financial capacity to deal with the core problem. It is a crux perhaps best exemplified by the apocryphal story of the ageing career criminal being led away to begin his latest lengthy prison sentence. He turns to the Prison Service officer leading him off into custody and quips: 'You think I'm bad? Wait till you see what is growing up behind me.'

12

The Law

On 10 June 2008, the most senior and experienced criminal court judge in Ireland, Mr Justice Paul Carney, delivered a lecture to a group of young law students, solicitors, barristers and a few assembled victims' rights campaigners. In the Irish newspapers of the following day, his speech was duly covered but it did not generate banner headlines. Far from it. In three key newspapers – the *Irish Independent*, *The Irish Times* and the *Irish Examiner* – it merited, on average, little more than fourteen paragraphs on an inside page. The papers were instead dominated by the build-up to the EU Lisbon Treaty referendum and the blockade of Irish ports by income-hit fishermen.

Yet what was most remarkable about that was the fact Mr Justice Carney had issued a stark warning about 'the mindless viciousness' of Ireland's spiralling violent crime rates. Specifically, he warned that knife crime was now virtually out of control Crucially, he raised the query whether Ireland's current sentencing guidelines were designed for a different, less violent era where drug-fuelled crime was unheard of. Coming from such an eminent criminal law expert, the lecture sounded like an effective wake-up call for society.

Pointedly, Mr Justice Carney said that had the Irish victims' rights group, AdVIC, been delivering the lecture in his place they might well argue that the judicial system was simply not dealing with violent crime firmly enough. 'So far as willful, violent, gratuitous homicides are concerned the courts are not dealing with them with the severity expected by the majority of right-thinking members of society who are fearful for their personal safety.'

Mr Justice Carney said that AdVIC and the families of homicide victims want to know why this is so – and he is simply not in a position to answer that question. 'I think it may have something to do with the rules being formulated in different times.' Critically, he said that some legal guidelines from previous Court of Criminal Appeal cases were handed down in a very different era. '[They] do not compare with the mindless viciousness of what is going through the courts today – drug crime did not of course exist and alcohol probably not much more than the messy drunk.'

He stressed that the case of changing the fundamental principles of sentencing policy rests not with the Central Criminal Court – the criminal arm of the High Court – but, rather, with the Supreme Court and the Court of Criminal Appeal.

Several aspects of the lecture were important, not least that it warranted greater media coverage than it actually garnered. Firstly, Ireland's most experienced criminal court judge was sounding the alarm bell over the rate of violent crime now pouring through courtroom doors nationwide. Secondly, he was raising question marks over sentencing policies and guidelines being both outmoded and outdated. Thirdly, he was also raising the issue of reform of those self-same sentencing guidelines. In the audience, several members of AdVIC listened attentively – and later endorsed views that they had themselves been espousing for years, i.e. that Ireland's treatment of violent offenders falls far short of what it should be.

Lastly, and perhaps most significantly, Mr Justice Carney specifically mentioned AdVIC in his lecture. This in itself was proof positive of just how much the scales of justice have begun to tilt to recognise both crime victims and their families. For decades, families felt themselves to be little more than silent, powerless observers of a process that often left them bruised, battered and frustrated. In several high profile cases, victims and their families had warned that the legal process caused them almost as much pain as the initial crime itself. Perhaps most wounding of all, some families felt that the law served as more of a protection to offenders than their victims. This is perhaps unfair but it reflects the view of a significant number of people exiting the criminal justice system.

What few in the august surroundings of UCC's Aula Maxima that night would have guessed was that the lecture would also have an unexpected judicial consequence two years later. Two men – convicted of knife killing – were subsequently granted a full retrial by the Court of Criminal Appeal after they cited the very lecture delivered by Mr Justice Carney as a factor in making their conviction 'unsafe'. The Court of Criminal Appeal agreed and the retrial is now pending.

From the early 1990s, the victims of violent crime and their families suddenly began to find that their voices carried much greater weight within the Irish judicial system. Victims always figured in judicial calculations – it is patently wrong to suggest that victims and their families were ever forgotten by the law. But the law now seemed to be waking up to the fact many people in society felt the judicial process was not treating violent crime harshly enough and that, in the necessary drive to foster the rehabilitation of offenders, the entitlements of victims and their families had, at times, taken a back seat.

This was partly triggered by a number of high-profile criminal cases where the media – and society in general – reacted with outrage to the manner in which some violent offenders were dealt with through sentences perceived to be excessively lenient. On other occasions – such as notorious Wicklow rapist Larry Murphy – the law seemed powerless to deal with an individual suspected of involvement in other attacks but for whom prosecutions had proved an evidential impossibility.

In Murphy's case, his release from Arbour Hill Prison on 12 August 2010 triggered a near-hysterical debate within sections of the tabloid media over sentencing policy, the protection of society from convicted sex offenders and the sentence remission system.

Justice Minister Dermot Ahern went to great pains on both RTÉ and TV3 to stress that Murphy was not released early. He had served his sentence in the eyes of the law. While this was patently correct, there was palpable unease over the fact Murphy had received a fifteen-year sentence in 2000 for the brutal rape, abduction and attempted murder of a young Carlow businesswoman. But he ultimately served just ten and a half years – because he was entitled to 25 per cent remission of his sentence for his good behaviour while in custody.

However, the latter came under intense scrutiny when it emerged that Murphy had repeatedly refused to cooperate with all treatment options offered to sex offenders. Murphy had also been repeatedly interviewed by Gardaí, while in custody, in relation to several high-profile cases of missing women in the midlands and Dublin Mountain but did not provide any material assistance.

There was further outrage when it emerged that, after his release, Murphy had seven full days to notify Gardaí of his intended address under the terms of the Register of Sex Offenders to which he was bound. Gardaí knew where Murphy was – but ordinary householders found themselves caught in a vortex of fear over the location of Ireland's most feared sex predator. The tabloid media dubbed Murphy 'The Beast of Baltinglass' and Sinn Féin even organised meetings in his own community so that people could voice their concerns. It all merely added to the pervading sense of fear.

Murphy's own family spoke of their horror at what he had done and their concerns about any attempt by him to return to the closely knit Wicklow community. One 31-year-old woman told the *Irish Independent* she was living in fear and felt that she now needed a chaperone if she intended to go out at night.

In the end, Gardaí were effectively prompted to give Murphy temporary protection after even State-operated halfway houses began to be the focus of major public protests amid local rumours Murphy was resident there. Hardly surprisingly, Murphy opted to move to Spain in a bid to build a new life and escape the intense glare of publicity.

But the Murphy controversy once again highlighted the contrasts within the legal system. There were perceived to be substantial supports available for Murphy when he was released from jail – but sex crime victims often have to rely on voluntary groups such as Rape Crisis Centres for their supports. With the noted – and honorable – exception of the Gardaí, the law does not provide a lot of supports for victims once the judicial process is finished. Sometimes, there is a chronic lack of support while the process is even ongoing.

A raft of changes have been enacted in a bid to try to redress the balance. Some, such as victim impact statements, gave a crucial voice to the families of violent crime victims. Others, such as the Sex Offenders Register, attempted to address clear shortcomings in the law's treatment of specific offenders and any ongoing threat they might pose to society. The greatest single success – as former Garda Commissioner Pat Byrne acknowledged – was the creation of the Criminal Assets Bureau (CAB), which allowed authorities to strip criminals of the proceeds of crime. No single piece of Irish criminal legislation in the past fifty years has proved as successful as the CAB. The legislation – introduced in the wake of public horror over the gangland-ordered killing of journalist Veronia Guerin in 1996 – brought about a 15 per cent decline in overall crime rates within the first eighteen months of its use.

The 'law and order' debate gained such traction in the 1980s and '90s that it proved the deciding element of the 1997 General Election. Fianna Fail coined the now infamous promise of 'zero tolerance' towards violent offenders in their General Election manifesto and, as Pat Leahy pointed out in his political analysis *Showtime*, beat the Rainbow Coalition to hold the reins of power through the Celtic Tiger years. But the legacy of 'zero tolerance' was underwhelming to say the least. Drug-fuelled gangland crime spiralled to new levels, Irish prisons creaked at the seams with overcrowding, and violent crime rates remained at alarming levels, eventually to surge upwards.

Yet, despite this, the focus within judicial circles increasingly dealt with how the law interacted with crime victims and their families. There suddenly emerged in Ireland two different views on the same issue: politicians, and many within the media, felt that the law needed to take greater account of victims' rights and to 'get tough' with violent offenders. But others, many within the legal world, felt that the law was consistently being pushed in one direction, that of the prosecution.

Mr Justice Carney himself underpinned the dynamic by devoting his initial series of lectures as Adjunct Professor of Law at UCC to issues concerning victims and their rights. The lectures ranging from victim impact statements to knife crime and from how modern courts deal with victims and their families to the reasons why judges cannot be overly sympathetic during trials to the families of murder victims.

His voice is not the only one to raise issues concerning sentencing policy and victims' rights. District Court judge Michael Pattwell has been an outspoken advocate of pioneering legal reforms and has also questioned the manner in which sentences from trial judges are amended by higher courts, querying what kind of message that sends out to offenders about the judicial system. He has also queried why judges who take a strong stance on crimes that society is clearly worried about then find their sentences regularly being amended and overturned by higher courts.

No single issue rivals sentencing at the painful fault line where the judicial system and victims' rights collide. Access to information, explanations from the DPP's office and even victim impact statements have all made headlines over the years. But nothing generates media headlines like the issue of sentencing policy – particularly the relentless tabloid campaign claiming that sentences for violent offenders are routinely too lenient. As in Britain, such campaigns sell tabloid newspapers. But they also generate a subtle and increasingly alarming perception that the law itself is not working properly.

It is an issue that judges are all too acutely aware of and regularly take the opportunity to point out from the bench that sentencing policy is a matter for the courts not for newspaper editors. Similarly, the issue of mandatory sentencing is something that rankles with some judges – particularly what is privately perceived as the attempt by politicians to tie the hands of judges when dealing with offenders in complex case scenarios. A specific example in point was the Oireachtas move, under Section 15 (A) of the Misuse of Drugs Act, to impose a mandatory ten-year prison sentence for those convicted of having drugs for sale or supply over a specific street value (currently €13,000). The legislation provided for specific exceptions where the mandatory ten-year sentence could be avoided – and those exceptions are now routinely applied by judges.

Unsurprisingly, the regular newspaper columns and radio programmes devoted to law reform are often greeted with grave suspicion within legal circles. In fact, some senior judges have taken the opportunity to publicly query the near-hysterical demand for sweeping legal reforms, expressing serious concerns about the long-term consequences of such actions.

In June 2007, Mr Justice Adrian Hardiman of the Supreme Court delivered a keynote lecture on legal reform in UCC – ironically, just metres from where Mr Justice Carney delivered his series of lectures on the law and victims. His address dealt with the latest political buzzword – 'rebalancing' the law – and he raised serious issues about the campaigns for some legal changes. He raised particular concerns about the 'Law Rebalancing Committee', which was examining the need for key reforms.

'The rebalancing committee, and on the very word I will have something to say in a moment, the rebalancing committee was a body of people not one of whom had five minutes experience of either prosecuting or defending in a criminal court,' Mr Justice Hardiman said. 'It was quite remarkable – it was as though the committee had been appointed, I would say many of their members, and of course

Prof. Wynn-Morgan and of course Gerard Hogan for whom I have the greatest respect, but they laboured under that single disadvantage. They had never prosecuted once nor defended once. Now that is an unfortunate drawback. Can you imagine a committee established on a health question with no doctors? Or an agricultural question with no farmers? Can you imagine any of those bodies tolerating it? Well, that is what happened in relation to criminal justice and I shall be submitting that it is part of a very obvious and very sustained procedure to change the assumptions as to criminal justice – to ridicule it in its present form and to rebalance, that wonderful Blair-ite word.'

Mr Justice Hardiman focused on how, at times, political demands for legal reform have come to mirror tabloid newspaper policies and campaigns – and that anything not delivering a conviction within the judicial system is now apparently to be viewed almost as 'a malfunction'.

'There is no topic in which more advantage is taken of a lack of public understanding. And there is a great need to explain many criminal justice topics in a manner which the media are neither willing nor able to do. The very phrase "rebalancing criminal justice" seems to me to typify the sort of phrase designed to obscure rather than clarify issues and to introduce concepts by way of assumption. What do you rebalance except something that is not working right? You have already made an enormous assumption. This is actively used by those who adopt a Tony Blair approach. I never thought I would liken Michael McDowell to that particular approach but here we have it used.

'It is such a friendly, cuddly unthreatening word – "don't

worry, I am just going to rebalance you, it won't hurt for a moment." Over the past number of years I have become gravely concerned about the tone and the context in which a lot of debate and discussion on criminal law topics has taken place. In the first place, it is one of extreme over-simplification and populism in relation to which, as an academic commentator, Claire Hamilton, in her book on the presumption of innocence, has observed some parliamentary contributions are indistinguishable both in tone and style from tabloid articles.

'Two developments in particular are noticed in Irish public discourse on those topics. The first is a tendency to assume that those charged with an offence are guilty of that offence. This was nowhere better summed up than in a campaign slogan by someone in the course of a recent election, I really cannot remember whose slogan it was. It said that the party in question would seek, if elected, and I quote: "Tougher Bail for Criminals." Now the fact is that those seeking bail are typically not criminals – they are persons resisting being imprisoned for up to two or three years, after all, while the question of whether or not they are criminals is resolved. But the slogan clearly suggests, and is intended to suggest, that the question of their criminality can be taken for granted. In this it is typical of a lot of public discourse. Despite the confusion which a loose phrase like that [causes] . . . it is easy to imagine the reaction in Ireland if Irish defendants seeking bail in the UK or US attracted a headline: "Irish Criminals Seek Bail."

'The difficulty of the assimilation of the state of being accused with the state of being guilty is that in a system nominated by an approach like that it is very difficult to find any intellectual scope at all for a proper acquittal. Accordingly, a state of mind grows up in which only convictions are meaningful results of the criminal process and acquittals are to be regarded as malfunctions or, at best, meaningless or false results. And an invalid result possibly caused by a technicality.'

He argues that those who warn that the law is simply not working properly need to exercise caution and examine the facts in a cool, considered way with full regard for the consequences of any changes. 'As I said, the word rebalancing is pregnant with assumption. One doesn't rebalance something that one regards as already properly balanced. One sets out to rebalance something which is out of kilter which is not working appropriately. Accordingly, the persistent use of the [word] rebalancing involves an assumption and one that is rarely thought necessary or possible to stand over with rational argument. The assumption, those of you can remember doing Euclid in school, there was always something required to be proved. Well, the "required to be proved" bit has been left out of this particular theory. Assume the criminal justice system has to be rebalanced. How exactly? How is this seen?

'Of criminal law reform over the past twenty-five years, Prof. Dermot Walsh has said, in a very striking phrase, it has been all in the one direction. Almost without a single exception in the favour of the investigator or prosecutor of crime and to handicap the defendant. The only exception I would think is that sometime in the early 1990s the defendant or his counsel was given or afforded the opportunity of speaking last in a criminal trial. That apart, we have had twenty-five years of legislation, approximately from the Act of 1984, which introduced detention for investigation, up until the present time, all in one direction,' he says.

He warned about rushed reforms and expedient judicial changes, quoting an eminent US judge. '[Some say] no respectable or mainstream citizen will suffer if we tinker with the rights of these criminals in the trial process. This is a pernicious falsehood – most fundamentally for the reason identified by Mr Justice Thurgood Marshall of the US Supreme Court. Judge Marshall had been the chief trial attorney for the National Association for the Advancement of Coloured People (NAACP) and had seen a great many outrages defending the rape and murder cases in the Bible Belt. In US & Salerne we have a passage that I quoted in my recent judgement in the Shortt case. Justice Marshall had this to say: "Honouring the presumption of innocence is often difficult – sometimes we must pay substantial social costs as a result of our commitment to the values we espouse. But, at the end of the day, the presumption of innocence protects the [innocent]. The shortcuts we would take with those we believe to be guilty only injure those who are wrongly accused and, ultimately, ourselves.'

Hence, balancing the demands for tougher action against violent criminals and the need to preserve and protect the rights to a fair trial leave many wondering just how effective reform can be. Some believe that outside pressure is required – and, in August 2010, Ireland followed the lead of the United States in launching its own version of 'The Innocence Project'. Prof. Barry Scheck, the lawyer who formed part of O. J. Simpson's successful legal team in his murder trial, launched the American Innocence Project in 1992 and, since then, it has helped force the review of hundreds of conviction cases. In the US, 258 people have since been exonerated of crimes they were initially convicted of – and 13 of those were awaiting execution on death row.

'One miscarriage is one too many. Ordinarily, it takes years to establish a miscarriage of justice but my expectation is that, over the next two to three years, there will be a few cases unearthed in Ireland,' Prof Scheck says. 'This is not about getting people off on technicalities – our projects are only interested in people who are factually innocent.' The team pointed out that the families of violent crime victims want the person actually responsible for the crime held to account – not an innocent party.

Yet, amid a mounting wave of gangland violence in Ireland, Justice Minister Dermot Ahern clearly felt that the judge-and-jury process simply could no longer cope with the challenge of dealing with organised crime – and he introduced legislation to allow such offences to be dealt with by judges alone. It was a landmark decision. While the State created the Special Criminal Court to deal with the threat of paramilitary violence, never before did the civil authority strip jury trials from the handling of 'ordinary' criminal offences.

This decision was also taken against the backdrop of sentences for serious, violent crime having got substantially heavier in Ireland over the past quarter-century. While judges and the judicial [system] regularly get hammered in newspaper columns over allegedly lenient sentences, the reality is that sentences have gotten significantly more severe for violent offenders. The *Irish Independent*'s security correspondent, Tom Brady, pointed out that in the late 1970s and early

1980s, some homicide sentences amounted to a period of between ten and twelve years behind bars. Now, killers who receive mandatory life sentences from Irish judges routinely face spending up to seventeen years behind bars. In some notoriously brutal cases, they face spending substantially longer in prison.

Yet sometimes the problems of dealing with high-profile crime are not created by the intricacies of the legal process and sentencing policy but by the simplest aspects of how the judicial system operates at grass-roots level. In Kerry, the failure of either Gardaí or court officials to notice or halt a procession of people queuing to sympathise with a convicted sex offender in a courtroom and directly in front of his distraught victim sparked a national outcry in December 2009.

Bouncer Danny Foley (thirty-five) of Listowel, County Kerry, was handed a seven-year prison sentence, with two years suspended, in Kerry Circuit Criminal Court after being convicted of the sexual assault of a 22-year-old woman in a car park in the town. The attack occurred in the early hours of 15 June 2008 after Foley met the victim in a nightclub. Foley initially told Gardaí he had 'found your wan' semi-naked near a rubbish skip in the car park when he had gone to relieve himself as he walked home at 3.50 a.m. However, security camera footage later showed Foley carrying the semi-conscious woman to the spot where the incident occurred. When the woman was detected by Gardaí, her jeans and underwear had been removed and she had extensive bruises and scratches over her body. However, there was no clinical evidence of a sexual assault. It emerged during the investigation that Foley

– who was celebrating his thirty-fourth birthday that night – had bought the young woman a drink in a nightclub and then insisted on walking her home despite her wish to be left alone.

In the minutes before he was due to be sentenced, a long queue of supporters, friends and neighbours waited inside the courtroom to shake hands with Foley and to sympathise. The queue passed directly in front of the victim – and left her emotionally shattered. She was later even snubbed by some people within the Listowel community itself – an incident that reignited the debate about how the justice system and society itself deal with the victims of sex crimes. Foley is now appealing his sentence.

The Circuit Court incident prompted Kerry Rape Crisis Centre (KRCC) to query how society deals with and then supports people who report sex crimes. 'She [the victim] has gone through a terrible ordeal and it has been very difficult for her,' KRCC director Vera O'Leary explained.

Vera said that the young woman – who still lives in County Kerry – is slowly starting to rebuild her life, which has effectively been on hold since that terrible day in June 2008. The KRCC director said that she personally never previously experienced anything like the roller coaster of emotions that the Listowel case triggered. 'I am working in this area for eighteen years and it was the most difficult thing I ever experienced in having to attend a press conference where a young woman who was the victim of such an attack had to speak out just so her voice could be heard. I was extremely saddened at the position this young woman was put into and I was also extremely angered over what had happened,' she said.

Incredibly, a similar problem then arose in the gleaming new – and extremely expensive – Criminal Courts complex off Parkgate Street in Dublin. Mr Justice Paul Carney said the new Criminal Courts complex had been widely hyped as 'a victim-friendly building' with separate entrances and rooms for victims so they could avoid all contact with an accused individual. However, to get to the witness box, a victim has to pass within metres of the accused in the open dock. Mr Justice Carney said the tension is manifest when the witness is called to testify – and it would have been far preferable to have both the dock and witness box located at opposite ends of the courtroom.

'The victims should be choreographed into seating that is out of the direct line of sight of the trial judge and jury – and by all means be brought to the fore after conviction for the sentencing phase.' Mr Justice Carney added that, ideally, he should not be able to recognise who victims are during a trial process but that, once a conviction had been recorded, victims could then properly and fully give expression to their feelings towards the accused.

It is hardly surprising then that some families of victims exit the judicial system feeling bruised and battered given that even a judge's attitude towards them can impact on the trial process. In one case, a trial judge described the mother of a deceased person – who was then giving evidence during a trial – as a victim. In a subsequent challenge, two murder-related convictions were set aside on the basis that the appeal judge interpreted the trial judge's comment as offering a seal of approval.

It is also no wonder that trial judges are now warned that

extending even the most basic of sympathies to the families of those killed by violent crime can have repercussions. As Mr Justice Carney himself admitted to a lecture attended by AdVIC members: 'A trial judge would not know what he was risking in extending even a basic courtesy towards a victim during the trial itself. Victims will not be aware of the pressures of this kind operating on the trial judge and think he is just being gratuitously cruel and unfeeling.'

Yet what often hurts victims and their families most is that, once the criminal process is over, they feel forgotten by society and the judicial agencies. In most cases, victims' families have to organise their own counselling and then pay for it unless a support group or charity agrees to help defray the costs. In cases where a conviction is returned, support usually involves Gardaí – on their own volition and sometimes even on their own time – meeting families to check if they are all right or if they need any further information.

It is a harsh pill to swallow for families that, while they are left to rebuild shattered lives with little or no State help, the person responsible for their pain and suffering is able to call on a range of State services while in custody, ranging from medical, psychiatric, educational and rehabilitative supports.

The flow of information is similarly problematic. Victims' families have no automatic right to be notified of the early release of the person responsible for their loved ones death or injury. Currently, they must write to the authorities themselves asking to be notified. In some cases, relatives were appalled to come face to face on the street with the individual responsible for their loved ones' death or injury – without any prior warning that the person had even been released.

Such problems are now slowly being addressed – but victims' rights groups want the pace of change to be vastly accelerated while accepting that the legal system's careful checks and balances need to be respected. Says one grieving mother: 'We're not asking for the moon – all we want is a bit of information and for justice to be done. We lost loved ones – and we won't get them back. The law cannot right the wrong that was done to us. All we are left with is the hope that the law will do right by us. That's not an awful lot to ask – is it?'

13

The Prisons

In the twenty-first century, Ireland, like most of the western world, is still struggling to solve the problem that confronted the Victorians as they evolved the modern, humane penal system: how to strike a balance between the punishment and reform of violent criminals with the protection of society and the delivery of justice.

Under penal reformers in Britain in the late nineteenth century, prisons began the inexorable shift from places of unspeakable hardship, cruelty and punishment, up to and including execution, to places of confinement and, ideally, re-education and reform. By the time capital punishment – the last vestige of the old medieval penal code – became redundant in Ireland and Britain in the 1950s, prisons focused increasingly on helping offenders put past criminal behaviour behind them and encouraged their reintegration into society.

By the 1960s and 1970s, few openly questioned the policy of using prisons to help reform offenders as much as to punish them for past offences. Initiatives were undertaken to target low-risk offenders in open or minimum-security prisons. Prisons were also provided with expanded education and training units in the hope that inmates could productively use their time in captivity – and, when they eventually emerged from their completed sentences with new skills, could prove useful members of society.

It was perhaps inevitable that, amid all the focus on reform, the punishment element of the penal system became less fashionable. In Ireland, the 25 per cent reduction in sentence length for 'good behaviour' while in custody also became a cornerstone of judicial policy – as much to help the Irish Prison Service (IPS) by encouraging inmates to behave themselves behind bars as to offer prisoners a 'ray of light' at the end of their sentence.

Yet the problems now facing the IPS are daunting in the extreme. They have too many prisoners, too little space, ageing prisons and insufficient capital resources to build the new 'super-prisons' that were signalled over the past decade. In May 2010, Ireland's prison population surged over the 5,000-inmate mark for the first time in the modern era. The Irish Prison Officers Association (IPOA) repeatedly warned that their members were being placed under extreme strain by a chronically overcrowded and underfunded system.

Most worrying of all was the fact that far from proving to be places of re-education and reintegration, there was mounting evidence that some jails, due to a variety of factors, were becoming little more than criminal colleges. Some inmates served sentences for relatively minor offences only to return to jail a few months later on far more serious charges – largely as a result of contacts, information or skills they had acquired during their earlier sentence. In some cases, prisoners emerged from custody with drug habits that had radically worsened.

So grave are the problems now facing the prison system that even issues such as drug availability within jails have effective rivals for tabloid headlines. It took the revelations about the material smuggled into Irish prisons – ranging from mobile phones to a pet canary and from high-tech audio-visual equipment to pornography in 2008/2009 – to sufficiently shock an Irish public largely inured to drug use within jails.

The answer proposed by the Fianna Fáil–Progressive Democrat government in the 29th Dáil was a series of new 'super-prisons' to replace the Victorian-era prisons that were still the bulwark of Ireland's penal system. These would be self-contained, state-of-the-art facilities offering maximum-security detention for prisoners. Drug smuggling would be eliminated by seamless perimeters and costs would be saved through the use of in-prison court appearances via video-link, avoiding the expensive use of inmate transfers by Prison Service escorts to courtrooms the length and breadth of the country. In fact, the planned complexes are more 'prison campuses' than 'super-prisons'. Thornton Hall – where it was originally proposed to build four prisons – would effectively have replaced the entire Mountjoy complex in Dublin.

Yet the new super-prisons proposed for Thornton Hall

and Kilworth in north Cork soon threatened to become fast-fading memories of the Celtic Tiger era. Thornton Hall was initially cancelled in 2009 after the government raised concerns about the value-for-money on offer in the Public Private Partnership (PPP) agreement involved despite the fact the land-bank had already been secured. The government, faced by the worst recession in Irish history, decided it simply could not afford the 25-year cost to the taxpayer of the proposed PPP deal.

When Justice Minister Dermot Ahern unveiled a radically revised blueprint for the super-prison in July 2010, it caused outrage and was described by Labour's Justice Spokesman, Deputy Pat Rabbitte, as 'one of the most expensive, misconceived and poorly planned projects in the history of the State'. Instead of the 2,000-cell prison initially proposed, Thornton Hall will now have just 1,400 cells for 2,200 inmates. Instead of four prison blocks, the government was now sanctioning just two. Critically, the prison will now be developed on a much slower, phased basis – with the first phase, due for completion by 2014, providing just 400 cells for 700 inmates. When that is completed, it is expected that Mountjoy's male prison complex – undoubtedly the most problematic detention facility in the State – will be wound down.

Minister Ahern, when challenged about the fact the new 'super-prison' will still include double occupancy cells, merely replied that he felt it was 'a bit much' for each individual inmate to have a cell of his own. The prison is not likely to reach its full 2,200 inmate capacity until 2020 – or later if Ireland's Exchequer returns don't improve. Crucially, the radically slower development of Thornton Hall will mean the rest of Mountjoy, already described as one of the most outdated prisons in Europe, will remain in operation for at least another decade.

The problems at Mountjoy were underlined by the revelation in August 2010 in a study indicating that 75 per cent of inmates had taken drugs. Of Mountjoy's 700 prisoners, almost 500 were believed to have used drugs. In the first six months of 2010, Prison Service personnel had made 356 drug finds and confiscated 86 home-made weapons. The prison's new governor, Ned Whelan, said there would now be a 'zero-tolerance' policy towards drug use within the prison and announced a range of tough new security measures aimed at tackling the smuggling of drugs into Ireland's largest prison. These ranged from a €250,000 security net to cover the prison exercise yard to prevent drugs being thrown or catapulted over the walls right through to special guard dogs to patrol the prison perimeter.

These measures were initially spectacularly successful. Mr Whelan stressed that they had substantially interrupted the flow of drugs into Mountjoy and had actually helped to ease tensions within the jail.

Yet Labour warned that the revised Thornton Hall proposal would haunt Irish penal reform for decades to come. Deputy Rabbitte said: 'This has turned into a shocking white elephant for which Minister Ahern and Michael McDowell must share the responsibility.' Fine Gael were equally scathing over the manner in which Ireland's future prison needs were being redesigned. Deputy Alan Shatter warned that: 'This government's ability to waste taxpayer's money is astounding. The final cost of this project could prove to be truly astounding.' Put in context, before a brick had been laid or a perimeter fence erected, Thornton Hall had already cost the Irish taxpayer €40 million.

In Kilworth, the proposed site of Ireland's second 'super-prison', the land-bank had also been secured – but this time at no cost to the Department of Defence. Yet the proposed super-prison was still mired in funding concerns and the realisation that Thornton Hall was likely to be given clear priority amid ongoing concerns about the Mountjoy complex. The reality is that the money to rush through the next generation of Irish prisons for the twenty-first century is simply not there – and Ireland will, for the foreseeable future, continue to rely heavily on prisons like Cork, Limerick and Mountjoy, which were designed and built in the nineteenth century.

Ireland now has more people behind bars than at any time in modern history – with the exception of wartime and periods of political upheaval. Despite a dramatic surge in the size of Ireland's prison population over the course of the past twenty-five years, opinion polls have shown that citizens still overwhelmingly regard the country as less safe than it was a quarter century ago.

In 1995, Ireland had 57 people behind bars per 100,000 of the national population. By 2006, that figure had surged to 78 people per 100,000 of the national population. From having one of the lowest per capita inmate populations in Europe, Ireland is now mid-table and slowly edging towards the top six places. In 2009, the rate of increase of Ireland's prison population was estimated at 14 per cent – a growth curve that has enormous implications both for society and for the Irish Exchequer.

A further key factor has been the scale of the economic recession – and the fact that prison remains a vital element of Ireland's system for dealing with people who will not pay debts or fines. In 2008, a total of 2,520 people were jailed for the non-payment of court-ordered fines or repayments. But, within twelve months, that figure has soared by 4,806 in 2009 – a hike of 91 per cent. Compared to the figures for 2007 (1,335 committals) Ireland has witnessed a 260 per cent increase in the number of people being jailed for non-compliance with fines or repayment orders.

Worse still, the cost of keeping inmates in custody has similarly spiralled over the past decade – particularly those deemed to require maximum-security custody. By 2009, the average cost for keeping an inmate in an Irish jail for twelve months was €77,222 per annum – a figure that had, somewhat ironically, declined by 16 per cent over the previous twelve months due to falling labour costs in recessionary Ireland. But the cost of keeping an inmate in maximum-security detention in Portlaoise Prison was nothing short of stratospheric, at more than €110,000 in 2008.

The cost to the State of keeping a murderer serving a life sentence in custody – an average of some fourteen years – is now an average of €1.1 million. Yet while the State is prepared to spend that sum on locking someone up, in contrast it spends an estimated less than 0.1 per cent on supports for the families of crime victims.

On 26 April 2010, the governor of the Dóchas Centre – Ireland's biggest female prison – resigned after warning that her position had become untenable. Kathleen McMahon, who ran the Dóchas Centre for a decade, said that chronic overcrowding and the implementation of measures in the prison without her approval had left her role 'completely impossible'.

Dóchas – like virtually every other Irish prison – had been required to cope with inmate numbers far beyond its design capacity. Dóchas was designed for 86 female prisoners but, in April 2010, was trying to cope with 130. In some cases, up to five women were forced to share a single room. In 2009, Dóchas ranked as Ireland's most overcrowded prison – operating at 129 per cent of design capacity. It was a familiar story with overcrowding endemic in Mountjoy, Cork and Limerick Prisons.

Ms McMahon – one of the most experienced executives within the Irish penal system – bluntly warned that she was left with no alternative but to resign because of fears that chronic overcrowding would so undermine the progressive prison that it would inevitably revert to the way it was years ago with 'self-mutilation, bullying, depression and lesbianism'.

The Director General of the Irish Prison Service (IPS), Brian Purcell, was forced to respond directly to the issues raised by Ms McMahon – and denied any suggestion that large numbers of the Dóchas inmates were low risk or should never have been given custodial sentences in the first place. Mr Purcell pointed out that, on any given day in Ireland's jails, an estimated 25 per cent of inmates are serving sentences for murder, manslaughter, conspiracy to murder or assault causing serious harm. A further 20 per cent relate to convictions for drugs offences.

The problems within the prison service have not gone unnoticed. Liam Herrick, the Executive Director of the Irish Penal Reform Trust (IPRT), says that the ageing nature of some Irish jails and the ongoing overcrowding problems now need to be urgently addressed. In the wake of Ms McMahon's resignation he warned: 'If the Governor of a prison says that she cannot do her job under these conditions, then the onus is [on the] government to address the issues of policy that have precipitated the growing overcrowding crisis.'

Mr Herrick's major concern was that the revised blueprint for Thornton Hall signalled that Ireland was merely going to expand its existing prison model – not tackle the major issues underlying the problems of recent years, including overcrowding, slopping out and underfunded rehab services. 'There is a very real danger that we will now get an expanded version of our dysfunctional prison system. The Prison Service has until now argued that the new [Thornton Hall] prison would provide high-quality single cells, each with sanitation and showers, and a new level of regimes and services. That the prison is now to go ahead but already planning to double up indicates that the emphasis is not on improving conditions and regimes but merely increasing capacity. Questions remain as to what plans are in place for addressing the chronic and inhumane conditions in Mountjoy Prison, and whether Ireland can afford an ever-expanding prison estate which fails to address the underlying causes of crime.'

Minister Ahern was blunt in admitting in June 2010 that the IPS faced serious problems – but he claimed it was an international rather than an isolated Irish problem. In that regard he is certainly correct – both the UK and US are struggling to deal with soaring prison populations and the resultant costs to the Exchequer. Minister Ahern argued that there had been a consistent increase in the total prisoner population in Ireland over recent years, but that the IPS must continue to accept all committals sent by the Irish courts.

'This is due primarily to the additional resources provided by this government to the Garda resulting in increasing numbers of successful prosecutions and extra court sittings leading to more committals. There is no opt-out. Indeed the problem of overcrowding is not unique to this country. It is an international problem,' he said.

But such an explanation met with little sympathy from those working within the penal system. Prison officers, for one, were scathing in the criticism of the government's handling of the entire system. Irish Prison Officers Association (IPOA) boss Jim Mitchell was so appalled by the overcrowding crisis that he was moved to warn that Ireland simply had no plan to deal with packed jails now struggling to cope with inmate numbers they were never designed for. His primary concern was that prison officers were at increasing risk of injury because of the jail overcrowding and the disturbances inevitably caused. Mr Mitchell warned that already overcrowded prisons in Dublin, Cork and Limerick were now effectively being asked to handle 10 per cent more inmates.

'As it is, every prison in the State is bursting at the seams – it is a very bad situation,' Mr Mitchell said. Worse still, the profile of inmates in Irish jails has changed – with many vastly more likely now to resort to violence for seemingly trivial matters. 'They are a different type of individual and they resort to violence quicker than the old type, than your old "ordinary decent criminal" that they used to be called. It is a very different world now.'

On 27 July 2010, a snapshot statistical picture of Ireland's jails underlined the true scale of the problem. Figures published in national newspapers revealed that, of fifteen prisons examined, just three were operating below their design capacity. A fourth prison, Shelton Abbey, was operating exactly at its recommended capacity. A total of eleven prisons were operating over capacity – and, pointedly, the statistical picture came just weeks after a large number of short-term prisoners were released early due to accommodation concerns.

The problem for the Irish Prison Service is that extra jail capacity to ease accommodation pressure is only likely to drip-feed into the system. A new block at Wheatfield Prison has provided 200 new beds but the new Thornton Hall unit now will not be available until 2014 at the earliest – and that will provide only 400 new cells and 700 beds. Experts believe that is simply not sufficient to cater for the closure of Mountjoy Prison which, in July 2010, was catering for 867 inmates, male and female, some 132 inmates more than its bed capacity.

It also emerged that, in 2009, a total of €2.5 million was paid to prison officers in compensation for injuries sustained while dealing with violent inmates. A total of 112 prison officers were either off sick or injured due to inmate attacks and received compensation as a result. The incidents involved prison officers being stabbed, punched, kicked, attacked with needles and even, in several cases, having feces thrown over them by prisoners.

The biggest compensation payout was €500,000 for

a warden who was left permanently maimed by an inmate attack. In 2009, there were more than 1,000 assaults in 14 Irish prisons, 800 of which involved inmates attacking inmates and more than 150 cases involved prison staff being targeted. Riot gear was deployed to staff at Mountjoy on one occasion amid fears that an inmate protest over new security measures aimed at dealing with drug smuggling could escalate into prison-wide violence.

The mix within Irish prisons has also exerted pressure on an already strained system. In 1980, almost 95 per cent of people in Irish prisons were either Irish or UK nationals. In 2009, that figure had declined to 77 per cent of inmates being either Irish or UK-born. The remainder are from mainland Europe (13 per cent), Africa (5 per cent), Asia (3.2 per cent) and North and South America (1 per cent). The changing mix of inmate nationalities means prison authorities have to be conscious of accommodation arrangements, dietary and religious matters as well as potential flashpoints between nationalities that have outstanding issues between each other.

What is remarkable is that alternatives to the Victorian prison model have been available for decades but have steadfastly been ignored in Ireland. Advocates argue that these alternative penal systems offer not only cost savings to the State but a potentially substantial reduction in criminal reoffending.

In an article for the Jesuit Centre for Faith and Justice (JCFJ) in October 2006, Dr Mairead Seymour pointed out that Finland – comparable in both population and society to Ireland – had successfully moved over the course of twenty-five years from having one of Europe's highest per capita prison populations to one of its fastest declining. In 1975, Finland's prison population dwarfed that of its Scandinavian neighbours Norway, Sweden and Denmark. Now, Finland's prison population is 75 per 100,000 of national population – slightly lower than Ireland's but quickly declining. That has been achieved at the same time as a slight but gradual reduction in the overall crime rate.

Canada adopted a similar policy and, perhaps mindful of its jail-obsessed neighbour to the south, decided on key penal reforms. In 1995, Canada had 131 citizens behind bars per 100,000 national population – almost twice what Ireland currently maintains. But reforms adopted more than a decade ago has seen that rate plummet to 107 per 100,000 of national population. Again, it was achieved against a backdrop of a reduction in overall serious crime rates.

The key, Dr Seymour pointed out, is whether prison is regarded as a place of first or last resort. The problem for the prison authorities is not the violent criminals and killers who are serving long-term sentences but, rather, the pressure exerted on the system by short-term prisoners or remand inmates. Easing the pressure of the latter ultimately helps the prison authorities deal with the former in a more effective manner.

Worse still, the huge budgets required to deal with such a spiralling prison population and ageing infrastructure ultimately eats into the money available for programmes aimed at confronting offenders with the reality of their crimes and setting out ways for them to reform and reintegrate into society when ultimately released. The statistics underline the problem. In Ireland, an estimated 80 per cent of inmates are serving sentences of less than eighteen months' duration – with an astonishing 25 per cent of committals to Irish prisons in 2001 involving individuals who had defaulted on fines or court-directed payments.

The startling fact is that, in general terms, the Irish penal structure has not been drastically changed in over 100 years. Such high-profile initiatives as Anti-Social Behaviour Orders (ASBOs), Community Service Orders or even the electronic tagging of inmates has amounted to little more than tinkering around the edges of a creaking, monolithic machine that, for the most part, spits out repeat offenders. The budgets for the various services speak for themselves: in 2003 Ireland spent €301.9 million on prison expenditure. In contrast, it invested just €40.7 million – one-eighth as much – in the Probation & Welfare Service. The public sector cutbacks introduced as part of the hair-shirt budget of 2009 resulted in one Circuit Court judge warning that solicitors seeking PWS reports for their clients may have to wait between three and six months because of chronic staffing shortages.

The manner in which Ireland's penal system has become vastly overstressed has not gone unnoticed by the legal profession. Senator Ivana Bacik, in a legal address entitled 'Retribution or Rehabilitation,' pointed out that while repeated expert reports have advocated prison as a place of last resort, it has in fact become virtually a place of first resort.

She points out that, in 1985, the Whitaker Committee recommended that there should be a ceiling in Ireland for prison places of 1,500. Not only was the recommendation ignored but, by 2010, Ireland's prison population was more than 333 per cent greater that the limit specified.

'It is clear that the use of imprisonment is increasing at an alarming and remarkably consistent rate, despite the absence of any stated sentencing policy. In 1988, this trend in increasing committal rates was ascribed by McCullagh to the "increased punitiveness of the judiciary". He suggests this began in the late 1970s, arguing that the "unhampered operation of judicial discretion has produced a penal crisis", and that the judiciary should be subject to some external control in making sentencing decisions,' she says.

'His warning went unheeded. Between 1980 and 1985, there was a 50 per cent increase in the numbers sent to Irish prisons and this new higher rate of imprisonment was maintained in the late 1980s, despite the stabilisation and indeed decreases in crime rates. Between the years 1990 and 1995, the new, higher rate of imprisonment of the 1980s was further built upon, and almost 2,000 more people were sent to prison per annum in 1995 than in 1990.'

What is remarkable is that while Ireland's prison population is low compared to other European and North American countries, it is exceptionally high if considered on a rate of how many people per capita of the population are sent to prison over the course of a year.

Senator Bacik points out that, in fact, Ireland imprisoned a greater proportion of its citizens than any other country in the Council of Europe. The imprisonment rate was 328 per 100,000, more than twice the equivalent rate in France and Italy, due to the tendency to impose short sentences of imprisonment for relatively minor offences. Ireland continues to use prison as an option for dealing with relatively minor offenders – in 1993 some 35 per cent of those sent to prison were fine defaulters. The following year, 1994, one study revealed that almost 50 per cent of those sent to jail – some 5,398 individuals – received sentences of less than three months.

By 2008, the Irish Penal Reform Trust estimated that 62 per cent of all Irish prison committals involved sentences of six months or less. The problem is that, with the prison infrastructure now being severely stressed by the avalanche of minor offenders entering the system, there are fewer resources and opportunities for the prison system to focus on serious, violent offenders, their rehabilitation and, on occasions, assessment of their ongoing threat to society.

It is also clear that so long as the prison system is creaking under the weight of inmates – most of whom are serving short-term sentences – there is little appetite for expanding and properly resourcing community-based alternatives despite the obvious advantages of a lower reoffending rate compared to the so-called 'revolving door system'.

Bibliography

Asbury, Herbert, *The Gangs of New York*, New York (Random House, 1927 & 2001)

Collins, Liam, *Irish Crimes of Passion*, Dublin (Mentor Press, 2005)

Cummins, Barry, *Missing*, Dublin (Gill & Macmillan, 2003)

Davies, Pamela; Francis, Peter and Greer, Chris, *Victims, Crime and Society*, London (Sage, 2007)

Duggan, Barry, *Mean Streets*, Dublin (O'Brien Press, 2009)

Hickey, D. and Doherty, J., *A Chronology of Irish History*, Dublin (Gill & Macmillan, 1990)

Kerrigan, Gene, *Hard Cases*, Dublin (Gill & Macmillan, 2005)

Mooney, John, and Harrington, Jean, *A-Z of Irish Crime*, Dublin (Maverick, 2007)

Murphy, Ann, *Nothing to Declare*, Dublin (O'Brien Press, 2008)

O'Connor, Kevin, *Thou Shalt Not Kill*, Dublin (Gill & Macmillan, 1995)

O'Connor, Niamh, *Blood Ties*, Dublin, (Transworld, 2009)

Rae, Stephen, *Killers*, Dublin (Blackwater Press, 1998)

Reddy, Tom, *Murder Will Out*, Dublin (Gill & Macmillan, 2005)

Reddy, Tom, *The Murder File*, Dublin (Gill & Macmillan, 1991)

Reynolds, Paul, *Sex in the City*, Dublin (Pan, 2003)

Riegel, Ralph, *Afraid of the Dark*, Dublin (O'Brien Press, 2006)

Rieley, Abigail, *Death on the Hill*, Dublin (O'Brien Press, 2010)

Sheridan, Michael, *Death in December*, Dublin (O'Brien Press, 2004)

Waller, Irvin, *Rights for Victims – Rebalancing Justice*, London
    (Rowman & Littlefield, 2010)

Williams, Paul, *Gangland*, Dublin (O'Brien Press, 1998)

Newspapers

Irish Independent, Sunday Independent, Evening Herald, Sunday Tribune, The Irish Times, the *Star, Irish Mirror, Irish Sun, Irish Examiner, Evening Echo, Irish Daily Mail, The Imokilly People, Sunday World, The Daily Telegraph* and *The (London) Independent.*

Broadcast

RTÉ, TV3, TnG, Newstalk, BBC Northern Ireland, BBC Radio Foyle, C103, 96FM, RedFM, WLR FM and Radio Kerry.

Acknowledgements

This book would not have been possible without the support, cooperation and kindness of a great many people.

Shattered is based on interviews specifically conducted for this book, which I carried out as part of my day job as Southern Correspondent for Independent Newspapers or on source material kindly supplied by colleagues from cases that I did not directly cover myself.

I am greatly indebted to a number of colleagues for their kindness in agreeing to review the manuscript, for their helpful criticisms and for assistance with source material – all of which helped with the production of the book you now hold in your hand. In this regard, my thanks to Jonathan Healy (Newstalk), Paul Byrne and Dyane Connor (both TV3), Barry Duggan, Brian McDonald, Tom Brady, Dearbhal McDonald, Don Lavery, Edel O'Connell and Kevin Keane (all *Irish Independent*), Barry Roche (*The Irish Times*), Liam

Heylin (*Irish Examiner*), Ann Mooney (*Irish Sun*), Maurice Gubbins (editor) and Ann Murphy (*Evening Echo*), P. J. Coogan (96FM), Fiona Donnelly (RedFM), Olivia Kelleher (freelance), Michelle McDonagh (freelance) and David Forsythe (SouthernNewsNetworks).

While I am loathe to single out individual families, I am deeply grateful for the kindness of Monica Butler, Peter Keaney, Steve Collins, James Walsh and Sasha Keating, and the Bouniols. I should also point out that not all families gave interviews for *Shattered*. In those cases, all material used here is derived from court reports, victim impact statements, newspaper coverage of the trials and/or radio and TV interviews both before and after the judicial proceedings.

This book was the brainchild of The Collins Press who felt that many books, perhaps like the justice system itself, failed to give sufficient weight to the voices of families impacted by violent crime. Many 'true crime' books tend to focus on the crime rather than the aftermath. I am grateful both for being entrusted with this project and for the support shown throughout by the team at The Collins Press.

Special thanks also to Daragh and Mike MacSweeney of Provision, Press 22, as well as Cormac Bourke and Gareth Morgan of the *Irish Independent* for their assistance with the images included here.

Last, but certainly not least, I am grateful for the support of the 'home' team – my wife, Mary, children, Rachel, Rebecca and Ralph; my mother, Nora, as well as RoreyAnn, Craig, Conor, Cian and Caiden. Without them, this project would never have left the proposal stage.

This is my second true crime book. The first book taught

me that you don't write about such matters lightly – and that violent crime leaves a searing wound on some families that never fully heals. The pain etched on the faces of those left behind speaks volumes about the terrible aftermath of violent crime. 'Closure' is a word much over-used and misapplied in our modern society, particularly by journalists. However, in the context of this book I can only hope and pray that that is precisely what the families included in these pages find in due course.

If you have been affected by the issues raised in this book, please contact AdVIC:

email: info@advic.ie
Mobile: 086 127 2156
Website: www.advic.ie